Strategic Executive Decisions

Strategic Executive Decisions

AN ANALYSIS OF THE DIFFERENCE BETWEEN THEORY AND PRACTICE

Michael J. Stahl

QUORUM BOOKS New York • Westport, Connecticut • London

Library of Congress Cataloging-in-Publication Data

Stahl, Michael J.
   Strategic executive decisions : an analysis of the difference
between theory and practice / Michael J. Stahl.
     p. cm.
   Includes bibliographies and index.
   ISBN 0-89930-316-1 (lib. bdg. : alk. paper)
   1. Industrial management—Decision making. 2. Strategic planning.
I. Title.
   HD30.23.S725   1989
   658.4'03—dc 19   88-18666

British Library Cataloguing in Publication Data is available.

Library of Congress Catalog Card Number: 88-18666
ISBN: 0-89930-316-1

First published in 1989 by Quorum Books

Greenwood Press, Inc.
88 Post Road West, Westport, Connecticut 06881

Printed in the United States of America

The paper used in this book complies with the
Permanent Paper Standard issued by the National
Information Standards Organization (Z39.48-1984).

10 9 8 7 6 5 4 3 2 1

Contents

v

Part IV. Conclusion

Illustrations

Preface

This book was written for several reasons. Chapter 1 documents several drawbacks associated with much of the current research in strategy. Some of these limitations are: stretching historical data bases well beyond their original intended uses; poor cognitive insight into multiple criteria decisions; social desirability response bias in which subjects have a tendency to tell the researcher a socially acceptable answer in a direct question or interview format; lack of statistical rigor in analysis; and poor or nonexistent experimental design. These limitations are documented in Chapter 1. Chapter 1 offers a methodologically rigorous alternative in research on strategy of modeling executive decisions. Chapter 1 proceeds to outline the rest of the book by describing the classes of decisions which were modeled.

An allied objective was to bring together the many decision modeling studies which have been conducted over the last seven years with the help of several colleagues. Unquestionably, this book could not have been written without their contributions, and it is very much a reflection of their efforts. Richard Christoph of James Madison University coauthored Chapter 4. Mark Hanna of Clemson University and Don Parks of the University of Wyoming coauthored Chapter 8. Judy Holmes of Clemson University coauthored Chapter 10. Fahri Karakaya of Southeastern Massachusetts University coauthored Chapter 9. Kipling Pirkle of Old Dominion University coauthored Chapter 3. Rebecca Porterfield of Mississippi State University coauthored Chapter 7. Alok Srivastava of Georgia State University coauthored Chapters 5 and 6. Stanley Wallace of Reliance Electric coauthored Chapter 12. Thomas Zimmerer of Clemson University coauthored Chapters 2 and 11.

The manuscript was word processed several times with multiple revisions on the part of the authors by some very special people: Alfreda Bouyer,

Scarlett Nimmer and Robin Wilder. Without their competence and tolerance of my multiple revisions, this book would not have come to be, although, I must take credit for any errors.

A special note of thanks is due to my wife, Barbara, and our three daughters, Lisa, Shelly and Debbie. They understood me and supported me when I devoted many long hours to writing this book.

Strategic Executive Decisions

CHAPTER 1

Introduction

Over the last two decades, the Profit Impact of Market Strategies (PIMS) data base has stimulated an avalanche of research into corporate, business and market strategy. Indeed, Wills and Beasly remarked: "It is probably true that the PIMS program has produced the most comprehensive set of research findings available in the field of strategic planning" (1982, p. 434).

More recently, some have questioned the utility of further research using PIMS data by describing multiple shortcomings associated with the data base (Anderson and Paine, 1978; Ramanujam and Venkatraman, 1984). Ramanujam and Venkatraman specifically pointed out three major methodological limitations: "(1) data limitations affecting the choice of research topic; (2) data limitations affecting operationalization of constructs; and (3) generalizability and validity issues" (1984, p. 145).

These limitations apply as well to many other existing databases used in research on strategy which were not originally designed to test specific hypotheses on strategy but were resurrected ex post facto because the data bases were convenient. Poor cognitive insight into multiple criteria decisions, social desirability response bias in which subjects have a tendency to tell the researcher a socially acceptable answer in a direct question or interview format, lack of statistical rigor in analysis due to poor experimental design, and other limitations frequently hamper interviews and questionnaires in research on strategy. Indeed, Shrivastava recently remarked: "The field of strategic management has a vast body of practically useful insights waiting to be corroborated by rigorous research" (1987, p. 89).

This book proposes a methodologically rigorous alternative in research on strategy—modeling executives' strategic decisions with decision making exercises based on rigorous a priori experimental designs and multiple observations per respondent. It is an alternative which appears to be immune from the limitations mentioned, and possesses some additional strengths. This chapter lays the theoretical basis for decision modeling in research on strategy and explores the methodological advantages. Subsequent chapters describe several different studies which have used decision modeling to test specific questions on strategy with data from several different samples and instruments involving approximately 1,500 executives.

THEORETICAL RATIONALE

Several researchers have recently suggested that a way to analyze business strategy is through a decision making framework (Hatten, 1979; Hofer and Schendel, 1978; Mintzberg, 1978; Shirley, 1982). Hatten specfically remarked: "Although quantitative policy research has mostly been descriptive, it has addressed strategic decision making from a preconceived notion of what should be done according to the normative dictates of our theory. But, is that what managers do? Why not work backward from their judgment, explore stategic decision making as a personal and group process and develop new theory?" (1979, p. 460). The research studies in this book are not so presumptuous as to tell executives how they should or ought to make strategic decisions. Rather, the focus is to describe or model how they actually do make decisions. As Hatten indicated, such a plan may lead to the development of new theory.

Decision modeling, or behavioral decision theory, owes much of its development to the seminal work of Egon Brunswik (1956). He argued that a researcher could compute what is important to a decision maker by observing the decision maker process information on multiple variables in several decisions, and then by forming an equation which relates the decisions to the multiple variables. The equation is usually formed by statistically regressing the decisions on the variables. The regression coefficients from the equation are the measures of importance attributed to the variables. Hence, the importance measures are computed from the decision maker's decisions: the importance measures are NOT derived by asking the decision maker what is important.

The mathematical model associated with this approach is described in equation (1.1). Darlington (1968), Dawes (1974), and Goldberg (1968) provide detailed descriptions of the mathematical model. Extensive literature reviews may be found in Einhorn and Hogarth (1981); Hammond et al. (1977); Kaplan and Schwartz (1975); Slovic and Lichtenstein (1971); and Slovic, Fischhoff, and Lichtenstein (1977).

$$Y_j = B_1(X_{1j}) + B_2(X_{2j}) + \ldots + B_i(X_{ij}) \qquad (1.1)$$
$$j = 1, 2, \ldots, n$$
$$i = 1, 2, \ldots, k$$

Where

Y_j = value of the decision, e.g., an acquisition decision;

B_1 = standardized regression coefficient or importance attributed to the X_1 criterion or decision cue;

x_1 = the cue value or information criterion, e.g., the rate of return of an acquisition candidate;

j = the number of decisions;

i = the number of variables or decision cues.

The standardized regression coefficients (B_i) are derived from statistically regressing the Y_j on the X_{ij}.

In the case of an orthogonally designed and orthogonally coded experiment, the standardized regression coefficients (beta weights) can be transformed to relative weights (RW_i) by equation (1.2) (Hoffman, 1960; Ward, 1962).

$$RW_i = B_i^2/R^2 \tag{1.2}$$

Where

RW_i = the relative weight for cue i;

R^2 = the square of the multiple correlation coefficient.

Darlington (1968) refers to the regression weights as objective weights because they are objectively calculated from the person's decisions via regression analysis.

A third equation describes the use of subjective weights.

$$Y_j = SW_1(X_{1j}) + SW_2(X_{2j}) + \ldots + SW_i(X_{ij}) \tag{1.3}$$

Where

SW_i = the subjective weight associated with cue i.

The subjective weights are determined by asking the respondents how important the various cues are to them in making the decisions. Typically, the subject is asked to distribute 100 points among the cues in accordance with their perceived importance.

An advantage of the transformation to relative weights listed in (1.2) is that the relative weights sum to 1.0 for each decision maker. By multiplying the relative weights by 100, they sum to 100. This transformation to relative weights facilitates comparison among decision makers and comparison with subjectively stated measures of cue importance (subjective weights). Slovic and Lichtenstein's (1971) comprehensive review of information processing describes the comparison of relative and subjective weights as a measure of cognitive insight into decision making behavior.

Executives who make strategic decisions frequently communicate to other managers and staff specialists the decision cues and the importance of the cues. The others then collect infomation on the cues and report back to the executive decision makers. Thus, cognitive insight into cue use is vitally important so that accurate communication can occur on decisions which probably determine the future direction of the organization.

METHODOLOGICAL ADVANTAGES

Social Desirability

Some obtrusive research methodologies used in strategy research, such as interviews and Likert scale questionnaires, are prone to a social desirability response bias. This bias refers to a subject giving an answer to the researcher partly as a function of what the subject thinks is an "acceptable" or "appropriate" answer. The decision modeling methodology has been shown to be immune from social desirability response bias (Arnold and Feldman, 1981; Stahl, 1986; Stahl and Harrell, 1982). Given the lofty connotations of some terms in strategy, like "cost leadership," "white knight," and "greenmail," such immunity is valuable. It is left to the reader to guess if today's corporate raider will accurately indicate in an interview what he or she looks at when deciding to make a hostile acquisition.

Cognitive Insight

In their literature reviews, Slovic and Lichtenstein (1971) and Slovic et al. (1977) document the poor cognitive insight that most decision makers have into their own multiple criteria decision processes. The poor cognitive insight may be due to decision makers' reluctance to reveal their decision making models because then they could be replaced by computerized expert systems. Poor cognitive insight may spring from the fact that decision makers do not have access to that part of the brain which controls multiple criteria processing (Newell and Simon, 1974). Either way, the methodology of directly asking executives how they make multiple criteria decisions has limitations. An alternative is to statistically calculate how they make decisions by regressing their decisions on the decision variables. If orthogonally controlled experimental designs are used, and if the subjects are asked for their subjective measures of importance, then a test for insight can be performed.

Statistical Rigor

The decision modeling studies reported in this book used rigorous controlled experimental designs. Multiple replicates of factorials, full factorials, or fractional replicates of factorials were used. Thus, computations can be performed of the independent contribution of each variable to the decisions, as well as the interactions among variables. Since there are multiple observations per respondent, a separate equation can also be developed for each respondent. The statistical rigor associated with decision modeling contrasts with recent notations concerning the lack of statistical rigor in much research on strategy (Rappaport, 1979; Ross, 1978; Shrivastava, 1987).

Consistency

Decision modeling studies typically report high internal consistency measures due partly to their use of multiple observations per respondent. If a regression equation is calculated for each respondent, a test for individual internal consistency is available through examination of the individual squared multiple correlation coefficient (Stahl and Harrell, 1981, 1982). Such a test is seldom found in other research methodologies.

Individual Unit of Analysis

Much strategy research posits the contingency nature of the strategic management process (Anderson and Zeithaml, 1984; Hofer, 1975, 1976; Hofer and Schendel, 1978; Mintzberg, 1978). Thus, the individual executive in his or her unique situation should be the unit of analysis. Decision modeling yields an equation per respondent and thus analyzes individual decision makers. Alternatively, many questionnaire studies lump all decision makers together for analytic purposes.

Tradeoffs

Many strategic decisions involve tradeoffs or the notion that only one or a few alternatives can be pursued simultaneously. Indeed, Porter (1985) argued that a firm should pursue only one strategy at a time lest it become "stuck in the middle." Questionnaires or interviews which ask the executive about a series of alternatives with unidimensional questions do not capture the notion of tradeoffs. Decision scenarios, containing information on several variables at different levels as inputs to decisions, allow the executive to consider tradeoffs. Thus, the decision scenarios are paramorphic with the actual decision situation (Hoffman, 1960; Ward, 1962).

Paramorphism

Brown (1972) found that the policy models of individuals' decisions derived under natural and experimental conditions did not differ significantly. Therefore, simulated decision making exercises can be used to assess an individual's policy model.

Construct Validity

As Ramanujam and Venkatraman (1984) indicated in their recent literature review, data limitations in existing data bases frequently affect construct validity of the measures. The original design of a question in an existing data base may have been completely different than the use to which the data are subjected by subsequent researchers. Decision modeling exercises which are designed for specific studies seem to meet the requirements of construct validity for the variables under study.

Limitations

If something seems too good to be true, then it probably is. Decision modeling is not the perfect research methodology. Perhaps the biggest drawback is that it is a simulation. Although it is near field research in that it involves executives in their work organizations, decision modeling typically involves hypothetical decision making exercises. Since most executives will not allow researchers to be present and observe how they make multi-billion-dollar decisions which determine the course of their firms for many years to come, then researchers may need to suffer this drawback of decision modeling.

OUTLINE

Part I of this book deals with corporate level strategic decisions. The first study we did in this area of strategy and decision modeling is reported in Chapter 2 on acquisition decisions. This study demonstrated the utility of using decision modeling to examine an important strategic management issue. Since most good studies ask as many questions as they answer, this study was followed with another acquisition study. Then a specific acquisition model was tested—the Capital Asset Pricing Model (CAPM). Do executives follow the dictates of the CAPM concerning unrelated diversification when structuring their firms? Chapter 4 follows with another CAPM study. That study explored the CAPM and divestiture. As a follow up to these two studies on diversification, Chapter 5 examines acquisitions and strategic fit as ways to pursue related diversification. Using historical data, Chapter 6 examines which kind of diversification is more effective—conglomerate or related. Chapter 7 rounds out the treatment of corporate-level strategy research with a study on joint ventures across multiple industries and some observations on Chinese joint ventures.

Part II deals with business-level competitive strategic decisions. Chapter 8 opens with one of the most important business-level decisions at the heart of Porter's (1980, 1985) models of competitive strategy: How does the firm compete in the market? This question was asked of multiple decision makers in both the textile and printing industries including Chinese decision makers. Chapter 9 deals with a fascinating aspect of competitive strategy—decisions on entering new markets as a function of entry barriers raised by competitors. Early and late entry into both consumer and industrial markets are examined. Chapter 10 studies an increasingly important issue concerning the use of information technology as a competitive weapon across multiple industries.

Part III intensively examines strategic decisions within two organizations. Chapter 11 describes how decision modeling was used in a firm to measure the amount of disagreement concerning future strategies for the firm to pursue. Chapter 12 examines an important business-level decision in a high tech firm—the decision on which development projects to fund. The chapter also presents data which show how feedback of data on other decision makers in the firm can change a decision maker's policy.

Chapter 13 of Part IV closes the book with a summary, conclusions and implications for executives.

REFERENCES

Anderson, Carl R., and Paine, F. T. "PIMS: A Reexamination." *Academy of Management Review*, 1978, 3, 602–611.

Arnold, H. J., and Feldman, D. C. "Social Desirability Response Bias in Self-Report Choice Situations." *Academy of Management Journal*, 1981, 24, 377–385.

Ashton, R. H. "An Experimental Study of Internal Control Judgments." *Journal of Accounting Research*, 1974, 4, 143–158.

Brown, T. R. "A Comparison of Judgmental Policy Equations Obtained from Human Judges Under Natural and Contrived Conditions." *Mathematical Biosciences*, 1972, 15, 205–230.

Brunswik, E. *Perception and the Representative Design of Psychological Experiments*. 2d ed. Berkeley: University of California Press, 1956.

Darlington, R. B., "Multiple Regression in Psychological Research and Practice." *Psychological Bulletin*, 1968, 69(3), 161–182.

Dawes, R. M., and Corrigan, B. "Linear Models in Decision Making." *Psychological Bulletin*, 1974, 81(2), 95–106.

Einhorn, J. J., and Hogarth, R. M. "Behavioral Decision Theory: Processes of Judgment and Choice." *Annual Review of Psychology*, 1981, 32, 53–88.

Goldberg, L. H. "Simple Models or Simple Processes? Some Research on Clinical Judgments." *American Psychologist*, 1968, 23, 483–496.

Hammond, K. R., et al. "Social Judgment Theory: Applications in Policy Formation." In M. F. Kaplan and S. Schwartz eds., *Human Judgment and Decision Processes in Applied Settings*. New York: Academic Press, 1977, 1–30.

Hatten, K. "Quantitative Research Methods in Strategic Management." In D. E. Schendel and C. W. Hofer eds., *Strategic Management: A New View of Business Policy and Planning*. Boston: Little, Brown, 1979, 448–466.

Hofer, Charles W. "Toward a Contingency Theory of Business Strategy." *Academy of Management Journal*, 1975, 18, 784–810.

Hofer, C. W. "Research on Strategic Planning: A Survey of Past Studies and Suggestions for Future Efforts." *Journal of Economics and Business*, 1976, 28, 261–286.

Hofer, C. W., and Schendel, D. *Strategy Formulation: Analytical Concepts.* St. Paul: West Publishing, 1978.

Hoffman, P. J. "The Paramorphic Representation of Clinical Judgment." *Psychological Bulletin,* 1960, 57(2), 116-132.

Kaplan, M. R., and Schwartz, S., eds. *Human Judgment and Decision Processes.* New York: Academic Press, 1975.

Mintzberg, H. "Patterns in Strategy Formation." *Management Sciences,* 1978, 24, 934-948.

Newell, A., and Simon, H. A. *Human Problem Solving.* Englewood Cliffs, N.J.: Prentice-Hall, 1972.

Porter, M. E. *Competitive Strategy.* New York: Free Press, 1980.

Porter, M. E. *Competitive Advantage.* New York: Free Press, 1985.

Ramanujam, V., and Venkatraman, N. "An Inventory and Critique of Strategy Research Using the PIMS Database." *Academy of Management Review,* 1984, 9, 138-151.

Rappaport, A. "A Critique of Capital Budgeting Questionnaires." *Interfaces,* May 1979, 100-102.

Ross, S. "The Current Status of the Capital Asset Pricing Model." *Journal of Finance,* 1978, 33, 885-901.

Shirley, R. C. "Limiting the Scope of Strategy: A Decision Based Approach." *Academy of Management Review,* 1982, 7, 262-268.

Shrivastava, P. "Rigor and Practical Usefulness of Research in Strategic Management." *Strategic Management Journal,* 1987, 8, 77-92.

Slovic, P., and Lichtenstein, S. "Comparison of Bayesian and Regression Approaches to the Study of Information Processing in Judgment." *Organizational Behavior and Human Performance,* 1971, 6, 649-744.

Slovic, P., Fischhoff, B., and Lichtenstein, S. "Behavioral Decision Theory." *Annual Review of Psychology,* 1977, 28, 1-39.

Stahl, M. J., *Managerial and Technical Motivation: Assessing Needs for Achievement, Power and Affiliation.* New York: Praeger Publishers, 1986.

Stahl, M. J., and Harrell, A. M. "Modeling Effort Decisions with Behavioral Decision Theory: Toward an Individual Differences Version of Expectancy Theory." *Organizational Behavior and Human Performance,* 1981, 27, 303-325.

Stahl, M. J., and Harrell, A. M. "Evolution and Validation of a Behavioral Decision Theory Measurement Approach to Achievement, Power and Affiliation." *Journal of Applied Psychology,* 1982, 67, 744-750.

Ward, J. "Comments on the Paramorphic Representation of Clinical Judgment." *Psychological Bulletin,* 1962, 59, 74-76.

Wills, L. A., and Beasly, J. "The Use of Strategic Planning Techniques in the United Kingdom." *Omega,* 1982, 10, 433-440.

PART I

CORPORATE-LEVEL STRATEGIC DECISIONS

This part of the book deals with one of the most important questions in the strategy arena: What business should we be in? The answer to this corporate-level strategic decision can determine success or mediocrity for the organization for many years into the future. Failures in acquisition are frequent and very costly. Expensive subsequent divestitures at fire-sale prices often become the only solution. So why do acquistion failures occur so frequently?

The first study we performed in this area suggests an answer for the corporate planner and for the researcher. Chapter 2 demonstrates the utility of using decision modeling to answer the acquisition question of which firm to acquire. We found several significant differences between what the executives said was important in an acquisition decision, and what their decisions indicated was important. Is this lack of insight responsible for some acquisition failures? How can the executive communicate to long-range planners and developers which acquisition candidates to scrutinize for possible acquisition if the executive cannot accurately articulate what is important in an acquisition? How can researchers suggest acquisition models for executives to consider for action if their research methodologies are based on this lack of insight from interviews or questionnaires? This lack of insight into decisions is explored in Chapters 2, 7, 10, 11 and 12 with the same finding in each chapter. The implications are particularly relevant for corporate planners who must communicate with executive superiors and with other executives directing various divisions in the organization. These implications are discussed further in the last chapter of this book.

Chapters 3, 4, 5 and 6 explore another possible reason for acquisition failures. Are the dictates of modern financial theory embedded in the Capital Asset Pricing Model erroneously leading some executives to ignore the synergistic benefits of strategic fit and to pursue conglomerate diversification?

Chapters 3 and 4 found that executives do not follow the unrelated diversification precepts of the CAPM in either acquisition or divestiture decisions. Chapter 5 determined that attention to strategic fit in acquisition decisions is rewarded by the stock market in the form of higher price earnings ratios. Using historical data, Chapter 6 found higher profitability, higher sales growth and lower financial risk for relatedly diversified firms than for unrelatedly diversified firms.

Chapter 7 rounds out the treatment of corporate-level strategy research with a study on joint ventures across multiple industries. The same lack of insight by the executives into how they make strategic decisions was observed here as in Chapter 2. Lower return on sales and lower return on investment for the joint venture child were noted which suggests that joint venture as a strategy should be pursued with caution by the smaller firm in a possible joint venture. Interviews with Chinese managers and educators during a 1987 trip to Beijing, Shanghai and Wuxi support the findings of Chapter 7 concerning the importance of technology acquisition in joint ventures.

CHAPTER 2

Modeling Executives' Acquisition Decisions

ACQUISITION DECISIONS

As understanding of the overall policy field has progressed, several conceptual studies have been published that hypothesize the logic behind the currently popular corporate strategy of acquisition. Many of the criteria behind mergers and acquisitions have been discussed (Ansoff et al., 1971; Baker, Miller, and Ramsperger, 1981; Herman, 1976; Kumar, 1977; Nazem, 1981; Rappaport, 1979; Salter and Weinhold, 1978; Stotland, 1976). In general, the studies are normative in that they specify to the reader how a decision maker should make choices regarding acquisitions. No studies were found that *described* the actual acquisition decision making processes of the decision makers.

Because a descriptive acquisition study was not found, a strategic decision making framework has merit, and as multiple criteria are involved, multiple criteria behavioral decision theory was used to model and describe the acquisition decision making process.

Two major findings from the decision modeling literature are germane to this research. First, because of human limitations in processing information, most decision makers' policies can be represented by a few criteria (Newell and Simon, 1972; Slovic and Lichtenstein, 1971; Slovic et al., 1977). Second, studies have demonstrated that a linear model with additive terms, versus a model with multiplicative or interactive terms, accounts for nearly all of the explainable variance in descriptive models of decision making because few decision makers multiplicatively process information (Slovic and Lichtenstein, 1971; Slovic, Fischhoff, and Lichtenstein, 1977).

This chapter was written by Michael J. Stahl and T. W. Zimmerer of Clemson University. An earlier version was published in the *Academy of Management Journal*, 1984, 27, 369–83. Reprinted with permission.

These two findings, plus the knowledge from the acquisition literature that acquisition decisions are based on multiple criteria, led the researchers to the two primary research objectives of this study. The first is to apply the behavioral decision theory multiple criteria modeling approach with an orthogonally designed experiment to model acquisition decision making processes. The similarity or difference among the acquisition decision models is of great interest, given Hatten's (1979) remark concerning developing theory by analyzing decision making. The second objective is to examine the insight of the decision makers into their own acquisition decisions by comparing their relative (objective) weights with their subjective (stated) weights.

METHOD

The Acquisition Decision Making Exercise

This research assumes that an acquisition strategy consists of at least two major decisions. First, the firm decides to use acquisition as a strategy. This policy formulation decision is not the focus of this research. Second, the firm decides which candidate firm to acquire. This second policy implementation decision is the focus of this study.

Six criteria were predominant in the previously cited acquisition literature: relative price earnings ratio, relative purchase price, anticipated discounted cash flow, relative market share, relative productive capacity, and vertical integration. This research does not claim that these six criteria are the only acquisition criteria. There are obviously others. However, these are among the most popular and the cited decision modeling literature suggests that most decision makers process only a few criteria. The criteria were chosen to help examine the objectives of this research—the similarity among decision making processes, and the insight of the decision makers.

Based on these criteria, a simulated acquisition decision exercise was constructed. The exercise was designed around a one-half replicate of a full factorial experimental design. The 6 criteria were each listed at 2 levels for a total of 32 decisions per subject ($1/2 \times 2 \times 2 \times 2 \times 2 \times 2 \times 2$). The one-half replicate was constructed by confounding the 6-way interaction (Hicks, 1973). A fractional factorial was used to design an instrument of reasonable length, and to preserve the orthogonality of the criteria.

Figure 2.1 contains an example from the acquisition decision exercise. Subsequent to the example candidate firm, 32 hypothetical candidate firms were randomly presented in the exercise. Each of the 32 candidate firms was like the example firm except for the levels of the criteria. The first, second, fourth and fifth criteria were either HIGH or LOW. Cash flow was ADEQUATE or EXCELLENT. Vertical integration was NONE or SUBSTANTIAL. A copy of the entire exercise is available from the authors.

Figure 2.1
Candidate Firm

Relative Price Earnings Ratio. The ratio of the candidate
firm's current price to earnings for the last twelve months as a
percent of your firm's P.E. ratio is........................LOW
Relative Purchase Price. The purchase price of the candidate
firm as a percent of your firm's available cash and
borrowing capacity is......................................HIGH
Anticipated Discounted Cash Flow. The anticipated net
after taxes discounted cash flow of the candidate firm
for five years subsequent to the acquisition is.......EXCELLENT
Relative Market Share. The dollar volume of sales of
the candidate firm as a percent of sales in that
industry is..LOW
Relative Production Capacity. The productive capacity
of the candidate firm as a percent of total production
in that industry is..HIGH
Vertical Integration. Proximity of the candidate firm
to either your customers or resources is............SUBSTANTIAL

Indicate your recommendation regarding approval or disapproval of
this firm for acquisition.

      -5   -4   -3   -2   -1   0   +1   +2   +3   +4   +5
Strongly   Strongly
Against   Recommend
Acquisition   Acquisition

After the 33 candidate firms were presented, the subjects were asked to indicate the importance they believed they placed on each of the 6 criteria by distributing 100 points among them. The most important criterion received the most points, and so on. These weights are often referred to as subjective weights (SW_i) in the behavioral decision theory literature (Schmitt and Levine, 1977). A comparison of the subjective weights with the relative weights (equations 1.2 and 1.3) provides a measure of self-insight into decision making behavior (Slovic and Lichtenstein, 1971).

Because each subject provided 32 decisions, a regression equation was derived for each subject. The actual raw values of the decisions, which ranged from -5 to $+5$, were used in the regressions. Each subject's 32 decisions were regressed on the criteria after the criteria were coded as $+1$(high) or -1(low) to preserve orthogonality.

The Sampled Executives

The instrument was sent to senior executives at firms who had acquired another firm in the 18 months prior to this research. The names of the firms were identified from the *Mergers and Acquisitions* journal. The names of the executives were identified from *Moody's Industrial Manual* (1981) and *Value Line Investment Survey* (1981). In acquiring another firm in the past 18 months, it had been necessary for these executives to evaluate the criteria that they felt were most relevant in acquisitions.

Executives from 42 firms that had been identified in the *Mergers and Acquisitions* journal completed the exercise. The response of the firms was a pleasant surprise. Nearly all of the 42 firms exercised an option, identified themselves on the returned instrument, and requested feedback of their model and the model of the entire sample.

The firms ranged in size from $100 million to $7 billion in annual sales. Included were 31 manufacturing and 11 service firms. The specific decision makers included 15 presidents and senior vice-presidents, 24 heads of corporate development and planning, 6 treasurers or vice-presidents for finance, and a few senior analysts. All of these top-level decision makers had been involved in an acquisition within 18 months prior to the research.

RESULTS

The first step in analyzing the data was to check for the presence of interactions within the decision makers. Based on human limitations in processing data (Newell and Simon, 1972), only the 6 main effects and the 15 possible two-way interactions were examined. To check for the two-way interactions, a preliminary regression equation was computed for each subject's 32 decisions as a function of the 6 main effects and the 15 two-way effects. Of the 42 executives, 7 exhibited one significant two-way interaction. One exhibited two significant two-ways. The interactions were randomly distributed among all the possible 15 interactions: there was no preferred or consistent interaction. Even in the cases in which there was a statistically significant interaction, the additional explanatory power (increment in R^2) was only a few percentage points. Additionally, a group regression equation was computed with all 42 decision makers, 1,344 decisions, 6 mains and 15 two-ways. No significant interactions existed in the model of the 1,344 decisions. Because there was no preferred interaction, the increment in R^2 was small, and no group interaction exists, the remainder of the analysis is based on the 6 main effects for each individual regression equation. Therefore, the model tested for each subject was equation (1.1) where i (the number of independent variables) was 6 and j (the number of observations) was 32.

The second step in analyzing the data was to examine the reliability or internal consistency of the decision makers. This was done via an examination of the R^2 resulting from the individual regressions on the 6 main effects (Stahl and Harrell, 1981). An average R^2 of .80 and an R^2 range from .43 to 1.0 indicated that the decision makers were internally consistent in the application of their decision policies.

Table 2.1 contains the distributions of the relative weights for the 42 decisions. Two major points are worthy of note in Table 2.1. First, the means indicate that there are three categories of criteria in terms of relative importance. Market share was found to be by far the most important. It is almost double the weight of any other criterion. A second category of moderate importance was occupied by vertical integration, cash flow, and purchase price. Of almost negligible importance in this study were productive capacity and price earnings ratio. Second, the variability in the decision models, as measured by the variances and ranges on the relative weights, is dramatic. The broad ranges resulting from some executives giving a criterion zero weight, yet others giving it almost exclusive importance, are indicative of dramatic individual decision making differences. It appears that acquisition decision policies are firm specific or even individual specific. The decision policies certainly are not universal.

As a further check on the different decision making policies, the group regression with 1,344 decisions and the 6 effects was computed. The group R^2 was .39, compared to the average individual R^2 of .80 from 42 separate regressions. Thus, a dramatic increase is seen in unexplained or error variation by fitting a common group model. This is further evidence of firm or individual specific acquisition decision policies.

To try to shed light on the specific decision policies, a comparison of selected demographic data with the acquisition decision policies was performed. Six of the executives were treasurers or vice-presidents in finance. Two sample t-tests for these 6 versus the other 36 on the 6 criteria were performed. Of the executives, 24 were directors of corporate development or corporate planning. They were tested against the others in 6 two-sample t-tests. Of the respondents, 15 were top-level executives (chairman of the board, chief executive officer, president, or senior vice-president). They

Table 2.1
Distribution of Relative Weights

Criteria	Mean	Variance	Minimum	Maximum
P.E. ratio	2.9	18.4	0.0	22.0
Purchase price	16.1	666.7	0.0	100.0
Cash flow	17.7	489.7	0.0	92.0
Market share	36.7	965.3	0.0	96.0
Productive capacity	5.1	87.6	0.0	54.0
Vertical integration	21.4	653.8	0.0	95.0

Note: n = 42.

Note: The relative weights were multiplied by 100 to facilitate comparison with subjective weights.

were tested against the others. The 11 firms in service industries were compared to the 31 firms in manufacturing industries. The size of the firm, as measured by number of employees and also by annual sales, was correlated with the 6 relative weights. None of these 12 correlations was statistically significant. Of the 24 t-tests that were computed, not one indicated a significant difference. Tests of treasurers/financiers versus others, planners/developers versus others, top level executives versus others, and service versus manufacturing, all yielded no significant differences. In the absence of any significant relationships in the 12 correlations, and no differences in the 24 t-tests, the acquisition decision policies do indeed seem to be firm specific or even individual specific.

The insight of the 42 executives into their own decision making policies was tested via a comparison of the relative and subjective weights. Table 2.2 contains the means on the six criteria for the relative and subjective weights. It also contains the results of a within-person comparison of the subjective and relative weights via six paired sample t-tests.

The significant differences noted in Table 2.2 follow a bias pattern noted by Slovic and Lichtenstein (1971). Their literature review consistently found that decision makers tend to understate the importance they claim to give to highly important criteria, and to overstate the importance they claim to give to low importance criteria. This pattern is evident in the five significant paired sample t-tests between the subjective and relative weights. Slovic and Lichtenstein (1971) referred to the comparison of the subjective and relative weights as a measure of self-insight, that is, the closer the two, the more

insightful the decision maker was to his/her own decision making style. These 42 decision makers did not demonstrate good insight. However, a lack of insight alone does not demonstrate which set of weights is superior.

Table 2.2
Comparison of Average Relative and Subjective Weights

Criteria	Relative Weight[a]	Subjective Weight	t
P.E. ratio	2.9	12.6	8.61**
Purchase price	16.1	19.3	1.02
Cash flow	17.7	24.1	2.13*
Market share	36.7	21.2	-4.19**
Productive capacity	5.1	9.9	4.28**
Vertical integration	21.4	12.9	-2.57*

[a]The relative weights were multiplied by 100 to facilitate comparison with subjective weights.

*p<.05.

**p<.01.

Note: n = 42.

To determine which set of weights is superior, the power of each set of weights in explaining the variance in the decisions was examined. The explanatory power of two models, equations (1.1) and (1.3) was compared. There are 32 decisions (j) and 6 decision cues (i) for both equations. The models were compared by using 2 paired sample t-tests. The tests examined which model explained more of the variation in the decisions, person by person. The paired sample t-tests blocked on the individual decision makers and, thus, were within-person analyses.

Two paired sample t-tests compared the explanatory powers of the two models (Table 2.3). One test was performed for these sampled decisions and another test was performed for the population of decisions.

The squared multiple correlation coefficient (R^2) from each subject's regression was compared to the squared bivariate correlation coefficient (r^2) from the subjectively weighted model for each subject. Then, the squared adjusted multiple correlation coefficient (R^2_{ad}) from each subject's regression was compared to the squared population correlation coefficient (ρ^2) from the subjectively weighted model.

Table 2.3
Paired Sample t-Tests of Explained Variation

Model	Average Explained Variation Sample (Population)[a]	t
$Y_j = \sum\limits_{i=1}^{6} (SW_i X_{ij})$	.34 (.31)[b]	
		14.26*· (12.68*)
$Y_j = \sum\limits_{i=1}^{6} (B_i X_{ij})$	.80 (.75)[c]	

[a]The sample refers to the decisions provided by an individual for this research. The population refers to all the decisions that an individual could provide by completing the exercise several times. The averages are for all the subjects in this research.

[b]Averages of the squared bivariate correlation coefficients between the acquisition decision and new variables computed as the sum expressed in the Model column.

[c]Averages of the squared multiple correlation coefficients derived from regressions of the decisions on the acquisition criteria.

*p<.01, df = 40.

The R^2_{ad} provided a conservative estimate of explained variation for the regression models. It is a measure of the variation explained by the regression, corrected for the number of variables in the regression (Nie et al., 1975). The R^2_{ad} is analogous to the shrunken R^2, which is an estimate of the variation explained by the regression in the population (Cohen and Cohen, 1975). After an extensive Monte Carlo evaluation of the problem of inflated estimates of R^2, Schmitt, Coyle and Rauschenberger (1977) recommended deriving regression weights from the entire sample and then using a formula to estimate the population R^2 rather than splitting the sample and performing a cross-validation to estimate the population R^2. Cattin (1980a, 1980b) updated the Schmitt et al. (1977) research and offered the same recommendation. Similarly, the ρ^2 for the subjectively weighted model estimates the population explained variation (Cattin, 1980b).

In this research, the population and the sample refer to the decisions of an individual, because R^2_{ad} and ρ^2 were derived for each individual. The sample decisions for an individual are the decisions provided by an individual in this research. The population for an individual refers to all decisions that the individual could theoretically provide by completing the exercise several times. The averages in Table 2.3 are for all the subjects in this research.

Both tests in Table 2.3 demonstrate that the objectively weighted model explains the decisions better than does the subjectively weighted model. This statement is true both before and after shrinkage from the sample to the population estimates. In addition to the decision makers demonstrating poor insight into their decision making process, the application of the subjective weights produced weak models.

DISCUSSION AND CONCLUSION

After analyzing 1,344 corporate acquisition decisions of 42 executives who within 18 months of the conduct of this study had been involved with the acquisition of firms, several conclusions are offered.

First, executive decision making behavior on the implementation of corporate acquisitions can be modeled with a high degree of consistency with an additive linear model via behavioral decision theory. This was shown by the lack of significant interaction and the average R^2 of .80 for the main effects model. Therefore, acquisition guideline checklists, which are common in acquisition cases like White Motor (Steiner and Miner, 1977) and Dresser Industries (Thompson and Strickland, 1981), and which imply additive linear models, are better representations of those decision makers' decision processes than all-or-nothing lists that imply a multiplicative process. Additionally, this finding of representation via additive linear models coincides with much of the behavioral decision theory literature (Darlington, 1968; Dawes and Corrigan, 1974; Hoffman, 1960; Laughlin, 1978).

Second, the high variances and wide ranges on the criterion relative weights imply that the acquisition checklists should be modified to weighted acquisition checklists. The behavior of these decision makers demonstrates that the criteria are not equally weighted. Unequally weighted checklists are more appropriate. Nor are the criteria uniformly weighted by all the decision makers. Some attached zero weight to a criterion, whereas others attached almost exclusive weight. The weights to be used in a weighted checklist should come from the CEO or the Board. The process whereby the CEO and/or the Board specifies the weights could be very valuable. It forces the executives to think through strategic acquisition policies without the distraction of a specific acquisition candidate. The resultant weights also provide staff members with guidance on what information about potential acquisitions is critical and what is noise.

Acquisition policies are individual or firm specific. For the theorist, the firm specific hypothesis implies that acquisition policies are the perfect example of adapting a policy to the organization's environment (Hofer and Schendel, 1978). If an acquisition policy is firm specific, then it should be updated over time to fit with the organization's environment. The lack of association between the demographics and the individual policies reinforces the individual specific nature of the policies. Perhaps the best way to test this firm versus individual specific hypothesis is to model the acquisition decisions of several relevant decision makers within each of several firms. A test for variance within and among firms would address the issue.

The individual or firm specific policies may be partly a function of the acquirer's position. Indeed, relative price earnings ratio, relative purchase price, and vertical integration were all explicitly defined relative to the acquirer in Figure 2.1. Cash flow is implicitly defined relative to the acquirer's concept of adequate or excellent. Relative market share and relative productive capacity are not defined relative to the acquirer's position: the candidate firm could be in a different industry. It is noteworthy that of the two criteria that received the two highest relative weights, that is, market share and vertical integration, one is defined relative to the acquirer and the other is not.

Third, all the prior comments about differences notwithstanding, there is a common theoretical financial thread that can be woven through the relative weights. Salter and Weinhold (1978) point out that acquisition is the correct strategy when such a move will result in a return higher than the risk-adjusted cost of capital necessary to make the acquisition. They suggest that a company choosing acquisition as a strategy can create value for its shareholders "only when the combination of the skills and resources of the two businesses satisfies at least one of the following conditions: An income stream greater than what could be realized from a portfolio investment in the two companies. A reduction in the variability of the income stream greater than what could be realized from a portfolio investment in the two businesses—that is, reduced systematic risk" (p. 171). Similarly, Naylor and Tapon (1982) argue that the Capital Asset Pricing Model (CAPM) could be used in acquisition analysis. Indeed, after describing the value of a company in terms of the rate of return and the variance (risk) of the rate of return, they specifically comment: "The problem of the firm under this formulation of the CAPM is to select a portfolio of businesses that maximizes the value of the company" (p. 1168). Further on in their article, they remark that a company should strive for high returns and low variances of returns in building a portfolio of businesses. The two criteria that received the highest relative weights by executives in this study—market share and vertical integration—support the CAPM concept of risk-adjusted rate of return. These two criteria work to improve profitability and to reduce the riskiness of returns in the long term. Hax and Majluf (1982) demonstrate how higher market share leads to higher cumulative volume, which in turn yields lower unit costs and thus higher profitability. Thompson and Strickland (1981) argue that vertical integration can increase profitability and reduce the risks of dealing with suppliers. Conversely, the two criteria that received the lowest relative weights—price earnings ratio and productive capacity—do little to effect the long-term, risk-adjusted rate of return. Both criteria are relatively short term in nature. Therefore, the relative weights support the CAPM risk-adjusted rate of return concept if viewed through a time-phased lens.

The purpose of this research was not to test the CAPM. Rather, it was to model acquisition decision making processes. However, Naylor and Tapon (1982) described how a firm should make acquisitions in CAPM terms. Ross (1978) noted that although the attractiveness of the CAPM is due to its potential testability, no robust test of the theory had been performed as of 1978. As an area for further research, why not test the CAPM in a similar simulated acquisition decision making framework? Such a study would describe the candidate firms with criteria from the CAPM such as rate of return, variance of rate of return, and intercorrelation among businesses. Then the normative dictates of the CAPM could be tested, including the interactive or multiplicative relationship between the variance of the rate of return and the intercorrelation among the businesses.

The subjective weights in Table 2.2 do not support the CAPM risk-adjusted rate of return concept as clearly as do the relative weights. The subjective weights are more uniformly distributed and thus lose the long-run versus short-run distinction seen in the relative weights. It appears that the executives were making correct decisions, at least according to the CAPM risk-adjusted rate of return theory. However, they were unable or unwilling to verbalize the correct reasons in the subjective weights. This presents another reason to question the utility of the subjective weights. Therefore, merely asking executives which criteria are important in an acquisition study could be a problematic methodological approach. The acquisition decision process is not correctly or precisely modeled with subjective weights.

Fourth, the executives were making long-term or strategic decisions. There was little evidence of their using acquisition as a short-term or tactical device. Rappaport (1979) argued that acquiring a firm with a lower price earnings ratio than one's own can lead to the creating of instant stock value because the market suddenly values the combined earnings at the higher P/E ratio. Because these executives valued P/E ratio the lowest, they apparently used a longer term outlook in which they looked beyond the sudden change in combined valuations.

Fifth, the decision makers had poor insight into their own acquisition decision making processes. This was evidenced by five significant differences between what the decision makers said was important and what their decisions indicated was important in the relative weights. This coincides with the lack of insight reported by Slovic and Lichtenstein (1971) in their literature review. Nisbett and Wilson's (1977) more recent literature review indicates that one reason for the lack of insight is that people simply do not have recall access to the part of the brain that processes multiple criterion decisions. The lack of insight implies that one cannot just ask an acquisition decision maker what is important because he or she may not be able to verbalize the answer accurately. Rather, one should observe multiple decisions and calculate importance. This methodological point is one of this chapter's major conclusions. The regression weights explained more than twice the variance in the decisions than did the subjective weights. Thus, one must argue in favor of the decision modeling approach as a better methodology for measuring acquisition importance.

One also wonders if the reason why executives sometimes violate their own written acquisition guidelines, as in the cases of White Motor and Heublein (reported in Steiner and Miner, 1977), is because they have little insight into their own multiple criteria decisions. White Motor is now bankrupt, and Heublein subsequently divested itself of its ill-advised acquisition. One must wonder how important insight into strategic decision making behavior becomes. Hofer and Schendel addressed this issue: "Both practice and theory indicate that no exact calculus yet exists by which strategic decisions can be made. Instead, effective strategy making relies on the creativity, judgment, and insights of the strategic decision maker" (1978, p. 177).

Given that insight is so important and the decision makers in this research displayed such poor insight, one wonders if a form of cognitive feedback (Hammond et al., 1977) might be appropriate. They suggested capturing the decision maker's model by analyzing his/her decisions and feeding back the model, as well as the model of other decision makers. In such a fashion, the individual can start to consider, with the aid of the decision analyst, the appropriateness of the various models, the lack of insight, and so on. The reader may recall that most of the subjects in this research exercised an option and were provided with such cognitive feedback. Maybe the analyst can help the decision maker to achieve better insight.

One must mention a shortcoming. Obviously, simulating decisions in a hypothetical decision making exercise is not quite as good as recording actual acquisition decisions. However, the pragmatics of observation and the demonstrated superiority over subjective weights indicate that simulating strategic decisions via behavioral decision theory is a promising methodological approach.

To the authors' knowledge, this is the first study of strategic acquisition via behavioral decision theory. If several others (Hatten, 1979; Hofer and Schendel, 1978; Mintzberg, 1978; Shirley, 1982) are correct in their suggestions that a useful way to analyze business policy is via strategic decisions, then this acquisition decision modeling research may be the start of analyzing strategic policies by simulating strategic decision making behavior.

REFERENCES

Ansoff, H. I., et al. *Acquisition of U.S. Manufacturing Firms 1946–1965*. Nashville, Tenn.: Vanderbilt University Press, 1971.

Baker, H., Miller, T., and Ramsperger, B. "An Inside Look at Corporate Mergers and Acquisition." *MSU Business Topics*, Winter 1981, 49–57.

Biggadike, R. "The Risky Business of Diversification." *Harvard Business Review*, 1979, 57(3), 99–110.

Boulden, J. B. "Merger Negotiations: A Decision Model." *Business Horizons*, 1969, 12(1), 21–28.

Cameron, E. "Appraising Companies for Acquisition." *Long Range Planning*, 1977, 10(4), 21–28.

Cattin, P. "Note on the Estimation of the Squared Cross-Validated Multiple Correlation of a Regression Model." *Psychological Bulletin*, 1980a, 87, 63–65.

Cattin, P. "Estimation of the Predictive Power of a Regression Model." *Journal of Applied Psychology*, 1980b, 65, 407–414.

Cohen, J., and Cohen, P. *Applied Multiple Regression Correlation Analysis for the Behavioral Sciences*. New York: John Wiley & Sons, 1975.

Darlington, R. B. "Multiple Regression in Psychological Research and Practice." *Psychological Bulletin*, 1968, 69(3), 161–182.

Dawes, R. M., and Corrigan, B. "Linear Models in Decision Making." *Psychological Bulletin,* 1974, 81(2), 95–106.

Derkinderen, F. "Pre-investment Planning." *Long Range Planning*, 1977, 10(1), 2–8.

Hammond, K. R., et al. "Social Judgment Theory: Applications in Policy Formation." In M. F. Kaplan and S. Schwartz, eds., *Human Judgment and Decision Processes in Applied Settings*. New York: Academic Press, 1977, 1–30.

Hatten, K. "Quantitative Research Methods in Strategic Management." In D. E. Schendel and C. W. Hofer (eds.), *Strategic Management: A New View of Business Policy and Planning*. Boston: Little, Brown, 1979, 448–466.

Hax, A. C., and Majluf, N. S. "Competitive Cost Dynamics: The Experience Curve." *Interfaces*, 1982, 12(5), 50–61.

Herman, A. "Decision Model for Mergers and Acquisitions." *Mergers and Acquisitions*, 1976, 11(2), 14–21.

Hicks, C. R. *Fundamental Concepts in the Design of Experiments*. 2d ed. New York: Holt, Rinehart & Winston, 1973.

Hofer, C. W., and Schendel, D. *Strategy Formulation: Analytical Concepts*. St. Paul: West Publishing, 1978.

Hoffman, P. J. "The Paramorphic Representation of Clinical Judgment." *Psychological Bulletin*, 1960, 57(2), 116–132.

Kumar, P. "Corporate Growth through Acquisition." *Managerial Planning*, 1977, 26(1), 9–12.

Laughlin, J. E. "Comment on Estimating Coefficients in Linear Models: It Don't Make No Nevermind." *Psychological Bulletin*, 1978, 85(2), 247–253.

Moody's Industrial Manual (Vols. 1 & 2). New York: Dun and Bradstreet, 1981.

Naylor, T. H., & Tapon, F. "The Capital Asset Pricing Model: An Evaluation of Its Potential as a Strategic Planning Tool." *Management Science*, 1982, 28, 1166–1173.

Nazem, S. "What's in It for DuPoint?" *Fortune*, 7 September 1981, p. 64.

Newell, A., and Simon, H. A. *Human Problem Solving*. Englewood Cliffs, N.J.: Prentice-Hall, 1972.

Nie, N. H. et al. *Statistical Package for the Social Sciences*. 2d ed. New York: McGraw-Hill, 1975.

Nisbett, R. E., and Wilson, T. D. "Telling More Than We Can Know: Verbal Reports on Mental Processes." *Psychological Bulletin*, 1977, 84, 231–259.

Rappaport, A. "Strategic Analysis for More Profitable Acquisitions." *Harvard Business Review*, 1979, 57(4).

Ross, S. "The Current Status of the Capital Asset Pricing Model (CAPM)." *Journal of Finance*, 1978, 33, 885–901.

Salter, S., and Weinhold, W. A. "Diversification Via Acquisition: Creating Value." *Harvard Business Review*, 1978, 56(4), 166–176.

Schmitt, J., Coyle, B., and Rauschenberger, J. "A Monte Carlo Evaluation of Three Formula Estimates of Cross-Validated Multiple Correlation." *Psychological Bulletin*, 1977, 84, 751–758.

Schmitt, N., and Levine, R. "Statistical and Subjective Weights: Some Problems and Proposals." *Organizational Behavior and Human Performance*, 1977, 20, 15–30.

Shirley, R. C. "Limiting the Scope of Strategy: A Decision Based Approach." *Academy of Management Review*, 1982, 7, 262–268.

Slovic, P., and Lichtenstein, S. "Comparison of Bayesian and Regression Approaches to the Study of Information Processing in Judgment." *Organizational Behavior and Human Performance*, 1971, 6, 649–744.

Slovic, P., Fischhoff, B., and Lichtenstein, S. "Behavioral Decision Theory." *Annual Review of Psychology*, 1977, 28, 1–39.

Stahl, M. J., and Harrell, A. M. "Modeling Effort Decisions with Behavioral Decision Theory: Toward an Individual Differences Model of Expectancy Theory." *Organizational Behavior and Human Performance*, 1981, 27, 303–325.

Steiner, G. A., and Miner, J. B. *Management Policy and Strategy: Text, Readings, and Cases*. New York: Macmillan, 1977.

Stotland, J. A. "Planning Acquisitions and Mergers." *Long Range Planning*, 1976, 9(1), 66–71.

Thompson, A. A., and Strickland, A. G. *Strategy and Policy: Concepts and Cases*. Rev. ed. Plano, Texas: Business Publications, 1981.

Value Line Investment Survey. New York: Value Line, Inc., 1981.

Ward, J. "Comments on 'The Paramorphic Representation of Clinical Judgment.'" *Psychological Bulletin*, 1962, 59, 74–76.

Zedeck, S., and Kafry, D. "Capturing Rater Policies for Processing Evaluation Data." *Organizational Behavior and Human Performance*, 1977, 18, 269–294.

CHAPTER 3

Acquisition, Financial Diversification and the Capital Asset Pricing Model

ACQUISITION AND CAPM

Strategic management relies heavily on the concept of strategic fit in making decisions concerning the attractiveness of the various operating divisions of a company (Bettis, 1983). In contrast to the strategic fit emphasis, Naylor and Tapon (1982) and Mullins (1982) have proposed that the theories of modern finance, which stress unrelated diversification, might be useful tools in the strategic planning process.

The Capital Asset Pricing Model

The CAPM is a theory of the marketplace developed almost simultaneously by three economists: Sharpe (1964), Lintner (1965), and Jack L. Treynor (unpublished manuscript). The groundwork for the CAPM was laid by Markowitz (1959) and Tobin (1958) with their theories of portfolio selection, and also by Modigliani and Miller (1958) who developed a theory of capital structure and valuation. Since that time, many applications of the model have been proposed, aimed primarily at the individual investor putting together a portfolio of securities.

The CAPM is based on certain assumptions concerning the investor and the marketplace: (1) all securities investors are expected utility of wealth maximizers who choose securities on the basis of expected return and

This chapter was written by Kipling M. Pirkle of Old Dominion University in Norfolk, Va., and Michael J. Stahl. An earlier version of this chapter was presented at the 1986 National Decision Sciences Institute meeting in Honolulu and published in the *Proceedings*, pp. 1239–41.

variance of return; (2) estimates of expected return, variance, and covariance of all securities are identical for each investor; (3) money can be borrowed at a risk-free interest rate; (4) all securities can be marketed without significant transactions costs; (5) a tax-free environment exists; (6) securities are bought and sold in a perfectly competitive environment; and (7) the quantity of securities is fixed. The model proposes that risky assets can be combined into a portfolio so that the overall risk of the portfolio is less than that of any individual stock. As long as there is some difference in the variations of returns on the assets, combining them in a portfolio will always reduce risk.

The theoretical principles of the CAPM have been extended to the area of capital budgeting, and from there to the analysis of a portfolio of businesses owned by a corporation (Naylor and Tapon, 1982). This latter extension assumes that the various businesses have the same properties as securities. The CAPM tells us that the cost of equity, or expected return, should reflect the inherent risk of the individual business, rather than the parent company's overall cost of equity in order to be chosen for the portfolio. So, for example, when a firm is considering an acquisition, the expected cash flows should be discounted at a rate commensurate with the inherent risk of the candidate.

Two types of risk have been identified for any particular investment. Systematic risk is the unavoidable portion of the total, that part which cannot be diversified away. Unsystematic, or specific risk, is the variation in expected return associated with a particular asset and this part can be reduced through diversification. Research has shown that diversifiable risk is by far the lagest component of total risk, which appears to fit nicely with use of the CAPM.

The CAPM as a Strategic Planning Tool

A model for evaluating potential businesses for inclusion in a portfolio has been proposed by Naylor and Tapon (1982). A single corporation is considered whose stock is actively traded in a market consisting of n securities; the company is a decentralized conglomerate that currently owns m different businesses. Risk in this example is measured by the product of the standard deviation of a particular company's rate of return σ, and the correlation coefficient between the company's rate of return and the rate of return on the portfolio of all n firms, denoted by r_m. The authors chose this measure of risk because a company's risk is measured by its contribution to the standard deviation of the rate of return of the entire market portfolio. If one were considering only a particular company, a high σ might be undesirable. Yet, an r_m of zero would make this company more attractive, since virtually all specific risk could be eliminated through diversification. Any $r_m > 0$ implies there is systematic risk associated with a firm, which cannot be diversified away. This product, $r_m \sigma$, can be used as a measure of risk in discounting a projected earnings stream.

By subtracting a risk premium from the expected rate of return R for a company, the certainty equivalent rate of return is determined. The certainty equivalent rate is that return which equates a risky income flow to a guaranteed income flow. For risk averters, this guaranteed income flow is less than the expected return for a project. Risk premium is defined as $r_m \sigma$ multiplied by ρ, the market price of risk. The coefficient measures the tradeoff the market is willing to make for extra risk when increased returns are desired. Thus, the certainty equivalent rate of return required by the market for a specific company is equal to $R - \rho r_m \sigma$. In a perfectly competitive market, ρ is a constant. The risk premium implies that for every additional unit of risk $r_m \sigma$ borne by investors, the rate of required return increases by $\rho r_m \sigma$. Assuming the expected return will continue indefinitely, the expected value of firm V is expressed by Sharpe (1964) as follows:

$$V = \frac{R - \rho r_m \sigma}{i} \tag{3.1}$$

where i is the risk-free interest rate. Investment in the parent company is desirable as long as the expected value V is greater than the amount invested I.

This same analysis is extended to the divisions of a company. For each division j,

$$V_j = \frac{R_j - \rho r_{jm} \sigma_j}{i} \tag{3.2}$$

Where

V_j = expected value of business j;

R_j = expected rate of return of business j;

σ_j = standard deviation of rate of return of business j;

r_{jm} = correlation coefficient between rate of return for business j and rate of return for the portfolio of businesses (Naylor and Tapon, 1982, p. 1168).

The goal is to choose a portfolio of businesses that maximizes the value V of the company.

Brownlee (1983) corrected the definition of value in equation (3.2); the difference between two interest rates divided by a third interest rate cannot produce a dollar value. Naylor (1983) acknowledged his error, stating that R should have been defined as expected profit, not expected rate of return. Boardman and Carruthers (1985) question the conclusions drawn by Naylor and Tapon (1982), but their reformulation of equation (3.2) contains the same variables. However, no conflict was posed for this research, where value was measured by percentage chance of recommending acquisition, rather than by dollar terms. The original definition of R was used.

After introducing the model Naylor and Tapon (1982) then showed its usefulness for managing a portfolio of businesses. The risk-free rate i and the risk premium ρ cannot be influenced by management. But managers do have some control over the other three parameters. In applying the CAPM from a manager's point of view, one would like to plan a strategy to increase the company's rate of return R and decrease σ and r_m. The authors dismiss the management of R, noting that there are too many uncontrollable factors considering the company's many divisions. The proposed management of r_m consists merely of designing a portfolio so that this parameter is as close to zero as possible, or maybe even negative.

Controlling the variance (standard deviation) constitutes the justification of the CAPM as a planning tool. The total variance consists of the variances of each business unit σ_j^2 plus the covariance σ_{jk}^2 of all pairs of companies. To quote Naylor and Tapon ". . . the company should pursue a strategy of acquiring businesses with low variances (σ_j^2) and negative covariances of return (σ_{jk}^2)" (1982, p. 1169).

In summary, Naylor and Tapon propose the use of the CAPM as a strategic planning tool. The real message of the CAPM for acquisition decisions is to build a portfolio of business units with an r_m value that is close to zero or negative. Obviously, there are serious limitations to the real-world use of the CAPM as a strategic planning tool. Naylor and Tapon recognized these problems, and describe the limitations in detail. Yet, they proposed its use in conjunction with competitive strategy models.

Mullins (1982) suggests that the CAPM can be employed when considering acquisitions. In evaluating an acquisition candidate, the expected cash flows must be discounted at the appropriate rate. The CAPM can be used in estimating this rate, or cost of equity. Mullins offers the CAPM because it can account for the varying degrees of risks of the candidates, and so can adjust the required return to reflect this risk. He also discusses the shortcomings of the CAPM, but concludes that it is a useful tool.

A Strategic Management Perspective

A conflicting theory for diversification has developed in the strategic management literature. This approach promotes the concept of concentric, or related diversification, which maintains a common thread throughout the business activities. Strategic fit is stressed, in that a company builds on the things that it is already competent at doing. The result of strategic fit is synergy in some fashion. Thompson and Strickland (1981) identified three types of strategic fit. Product-market fit can be achieved when distribution channels, sales force and promotion techniques, or customers can be handled at the same time for more than one product or service. Operating fit involves economies being realized in areas such as purchasing, warehousing, production and operations, research and development, and personnel from more than one product or service. Management fit occurs when managers are given responsibility over areas that they have experience in; this allows the company to tap years of accumulated exposure from one line of business to another. The advantage of having strategic fit is that it provides a common focus for a relatedly diversified organization.

The use of strategic fit as a guideline for acquisitions contrasts with modern financial theory. In fact, in equation (3.2), a relatedly diversified company looking at acquisition candidates wants a high positive correlation r_{jm} between business j and the rest of its portfolio. The CAPM tells us that a very low or even negative r_{jm} represents the optimum candidate for acquisition, other things constant.

Bettis (1983) expresses concern over this conflict between the two theories. The value of a firm as measured by the CAPM does not include a provision for unsystematic risk, since it can be diversified away. The conclusion is then drawn that managers should not be concerned with managing unsystematic risks since such behavior will not be rewarded by investors. But Bettis points out that the managing of unsystematic, or firm-specific risk, is at the very heart of strategic management. The matching of firm-specific resources with opportunities in the environment involves the management of unsystematic risks. This type of strategic adaptation has been depicted in organizational theory as the determining factor for the survival of the organization.

Bettis uses the example of managing entry barriers, which might be used to deter the entrance of new competitors making essentially the same product, certainly a firm-specific type of risk. Modern financial theory would not be concerned with the management of this unsystematic risk, since the firm would not be rewarded for doing so. But many of the prominent writings in strategic management consider the building of entry barriers to be of primary importance (see Porter, 1980).

One of the misconceptions criticized by Salter and Weinhold (1978) concerning acquisitions is that unrelated diversification offers shareholders a superior means of reducing their investment risk. Empirical research provides little support for unrelated corporate diversification over a diversified portfolio of comparable securities with respect to risk reduction. If so, diversified companies represent no more to the shareholder than a mutual fund; these companies may in fact be less valuable because of higher overhead costs and lower liquidity.

Another misconception is that adding countercyclical businesses to a company's portfolio leads to a stabilized earnings stream and a heightened valuation by the marketplace. In other words, the correlation between the earnings of the acquisition candidate and the existing portfolio r_{jm} should be negative, if possible, as prescribed by the CAPM. This is merely an extension of the first misconception; the goal is to enhance the "safety" of the portfolio's income stream through unrelated diversification. The difficulty with implementation is that finding countercyclical businesses is virtually impossible. Similar to stocks, companies move in conjunction to some degree.

Salter and Weinhold (1978) suggest several ways for actually creating value for the shareholder, three of which relate to strategic fit. First, a diversifying acquisition can raise the productivity of capital when one merger partner's skills and knowledge of the industry are applied to the competitive problems and opportunities facing the other partner; this boils down to management fit. The second suggestion is essentially product-market fit: Investments in markets closely related to current fields of operation can reduce long-run average costs. The third describes operating fit: Business expansion in an area of competence can lead to the generation of a "critical mass" of resources necessary to outperform the competition.

This research addresses the described paradox between the precepts of the CAPM and strategic fit in relation to acquisition. The specific hypothesis follows: In making acquisition decisions, executives choose candidates in accordance with the postulates of the CAPM, as described by Naylor and Tapon (1982).

METHODOLOGY

The Acquisition/CAPM Decision Making Exercise

The methodology chosen for this study has been developed by Stahl and Zimmerer (1984). They used a policy-capturing approach to modeling strategic decision making. The acquisition policies of executives were modeled through the use of a decision making exercise, which draws heavily on the research from behavioral decision theory (Slovic, Fischhoff, and Lichtenstein, 1977). In modeling strategic decision making, one would prefer to be present for the entire process. Since this is not practical for examining acquisition decisions, one might ask the decision maker to recount the process employed. But as Slovic and Lichtenstein (1971) found in their literature review, decision makers have rather poor insight into their own multiple criteria decision processes. Thus, the justification for the use of a decision making exercise.

The decision making exercise represents traditional research in the policy area, but in reverse fashion. Rather than describe how a manager should arrive at decisions, this approach asks the manager to make a decision given a hypothetical situation. The decisions of the managers are then used to compute the importance of the criteria which are used in arriving at the decisions.

The decision making exercise used for this research was built around a group of hypothetical cases describing various levels of the cues suggested by Naylor and Tapon (1982) as being under the control of management. The first cue, R_j, is the level of expected return of business unit j. The second

Figure 3.1
Sample CAPM Acquisition Candidate

```
                ****ACQUISITION CANDIDATE #6****

For this candidate, the following characteristics are present:

---the RATE OF RETURN for this candidate is. . . . . . . MEDIUM

---the VARIABILITY of the rate of return is. . . . . . . . MEDIUM

---the CORRELATION between this candidate's rate of return

   and your company's overall rate of return is. . . . . .   ZERO

DECISION: GIVEN THE LEVELS OF FACTORS FOR THIS CANDIDATE,

          indicate how strongly you would recommend acquisition:

    0%    10%   20%   30%   40%   50%   60%   70%   80%   90%   100%

NO CHANCE OF                                        DEFINITELY

RECOMMENDING                                        RECOMMEND

ACQUISITION                                         ACQUISITION
```

---

cue, σ_j, is the level of variability (standard deviation) of R_j. Last is the correlation between R_j and the overall rate of return for the parent company considering business unit j, denoted by r_{jm}. The first and second cues have three levels: HIGH, MEDIUM, or LOW. The third cue, r_{jm}, also has three levels: POSITIVE, ZERO, or NEGATIVE. The result is a $3 \times 3 \times 3$ factorial experiment for a total of 27 different scenarios. Each respondent was asked to rate the chance of recommending acquisition on a scale of 0–100 percent for each of the combinations of cues. A sample is shown in Figure 3.1.

The Sampled Corporate Planners

The instrument was mailed to some members of the North American Society for Corporate Planning, Inc. (NASCP). This organization is composed of approximately 6,000 senior-level managers who are "in a management position in a large, multinational firm interested in keeping abreast of new corporate planning techniques and applications" (NASCP, 1984). According to NASCP information, over 60 percent of its members are involved directly with strategic planning in their respective firms (NASCP, 1984). Acquisition decisions are typically made by a group of executives which relies on staff support from planners such as these; no other staff group appears more likely to understand the intricate details required for an acquisition decision.

A total of 201 instruments were returned; 158 were properly completed, providing 4,266 decisions to be used for this research. The respondents had spent an average of over eight years in the strategic planning area; over half had spent more than five years as planners. The most common job titles were director of corporate planning, or vice-president for corporate development. These profiles indicate that the NASCP membership was well represented in the sample group.

Data Analysis

Based on the framework established by Stahl and Harrell (1982) and Stahl and Zimmerer (1984), a multiple regression equation was tested for each respondent to model the decisions of each executive.

$$Y_j = B_1(X_{1j}) + B_2(X_{2j}) + B_3(X_{3j}) + B_4(X_{2j}X_{3j}) \qquad (3.3)$$
$$j = 1,2, \ldots ,27$$

Where

Y_j = % chance of recommending acquisition for acquisition candidate j;

B_1 = standardized regression coefficient or importance attributed to rate of return;

X_{1j} = rate of return for candidate j;

B_2 = standardized regression coefficient or importance attributed to variability of rate of return;

X_{2j} = variability of candidate j's rate of return;

B_3 = standardized regression coefficient or importance attributed to correlation of candidate's rate of return with the acquiror's overall rate of return;

X_{3j} = correlation of candidate j's rate of return with the acquiror's overall rate of return;

B_4 = standardized regression coefficient or importance attributed to interaction of variability of return and its correlation with the acquiror's overall rate of return.

The actual raw values of the 27 decisions each respondent made, ranging from 0 percent to 100 percent, were used in deriving individual regression equations. The levels of each cue were coded to preserve orthogonality. Rate of return and variability were coded as +1(HIGH), 0(MEDIUM), and −1(LOW). Correlation between returns was coded as +1(POSITIVE), 0(ZERO), and −1(NEGATIVE).

Since there was a significant number of negative coefficients on the correlation term (B_3), all statistical tests were conducted on actual beta weights (standardized regression coefficients). But a transformed measure of the betas was also used for other purposes. Since the experiment was orthogonal, the beta weights from the regression equations were transformed to relative weights, which facilitated comparisons (Hoffman, 1960; Ward, 1962).

RESULTS

Each planner's set of responses was evaluated for internal consistency by examining R^2 values (Stahl and Harrell, 1982). High R^2 values indicate consistency in decision making while low R^2 values indicate a lack of internal consistency. An analysis for internal consistency was performed on each individual's regression model (equation 3.3). All 158 respondents exhibited internal consistency; none had an insignificant regression equation. Indeed, the average individual R^2 was 0.80, which indicates a high degree of internal consistency.

The hypothesis was tested by examining the individual regression models for equation (3.3). The significance ($p < .05$) of each term was evaluated. Only 2 of the 158 respondents (1 percent) were found to have placed significance on all four cues, indicating that the planners were not using the CAPM for acquisition decisions. Table 3.1 illustrates the number of significant responses for each of the CAPM cues.

The hypothesis was also tested by examining group regression results with all 4,266 decisions pooled based on equation (3.3). Only the first three cues reached significance at the 5 percent level. The group regression R^2 was found to be .58 for equation (3.3). Table 3.2 displays the results.

Table 3.1
Individual Results for Equation (3.3) for Acquisition

Cue	Significant* Responses	% of 158
Rate of Return (X_1)	155	98
Variability of return (X_2)	97	61
Correlation of returns (X_3)	68	43
Interaction between X_2 and X_3	3	2
Full CAPM model (all four cues)	2	1

*$p<.05$.

Note: n = 158.

Table 3.2
Group Regression Results for Equation (3.3) for Acquisition

Cue	Standardized Estimate	t score
Rate of return (X_1)	.734	73.85*
Variability of return (X_2)	-.197	-19.82*
Correlation of returns (X_3)	-.039	- 3.91*
Interaction between X_2 and X_3	.001	0.14

*p<.05

Note: n = 4,266.

Based on the results of the individual and group regressions, the hypothesis was rejected; corporate planners do not choose acquisition candidates in accordance with the postulates of the CAPM. The implication of these results is that the CAPM was not used as a tool in making acquisition decisions. These planners were instead considering the cues as individual factors in the decision making process.

The interaction term was found to be significant (p < .05) for only 3 of 158 respondents (Table 3.1). Nor was this term found to be significant in the group regression (Table 3.2). These two findings suggest that the interaction term adds little to the explanation of the variance in these planners' decisions. There is no evidence of a multiplicative relationship between the rate of return and the intercorrelation of returns among business units.

Based on the prior results, the interaction term was dropped, with the result being equation (3.4).

$$Y_j = B_1(X_{1j}) + B_2(X_{2j}) + B_3(X_{3j}) \tag{3.4}$$

The same tests were then run on equation (3.4). The distribution of R^2 values and the results of the individual and group regressions on equation (3.4) were similar to those for equation (3.3). The results with equation (3.4) are in tables 3.3 and 3.4. The standardized estimates on the first three terms were identical to the third decimal place for both equations, and the average individual R^2 value only dropped one percentage point to 0.79, when utilizing equation (3.4). The group regression R^2 stayed at 0.58. These results again point up the insignificance of the interaction term.

It is interesting to note that only 49 of the 158 respondents placed significance on all three terms. These results once again indicate that the planners

Table 3.3
Group Regression Results for Equation (3.4) for Acquisition

Cue	Relative Weight
Rate of return (X_1)	93.0
Variability of return (X_2)	6.7
Correlation of returns (X_3)	0.3
TOTAL	100.0

Note: n=4,266.

were making acquisition decisions based on individual cues. The basic cues of the CAPM, although significant individually in the regressions, were not used together as a tool in making acquisition decisions.

CONCLUSIONS

The purpose of this study was to examine the decision making process employed by executives in acquiring other firms. Specifically, the research was aimed at testing the use of the Capital Asset Pricing Model (CAPM) as a decision making tool in the acquisition process.

Table 3.4
Individual Relative Weights for Equation (3.4) for Acquisition

Cue	Mean Relative Weight
Rate of return (X_1)	77.6
Variability of return (X_2)	12.4
Correlation of returns (X_3)	10.0
TOTAL	100.0

Note: n=158.

Naylor and Tapon (1982) have proposed that the theories of modern financial theory be applied to the process of strategic decision making. These authors point to the CAPM as the vehicle by which the evaluation of acquisition candidates be made. The CAPM is a mathematical model which is grounded in the theory of efficient markets. It was originally formulated for the evaluation of purely financial assets, such as publicly traded stocks. The crux of the CAPM proposes that the assets of a portfolio be unrelated or, ideally, negatively related in order to reduce the risk of investment. This concept has been extended to the area of capital budgeting, and most recently, to the area of acquisition and merger evaluation.

In contrast, research in the strategic management area suggests that the concept of "strategic fit" must be considered. Strategic fit embodies the notion that operating divisions which are related in some fashion are desirable for inclusion in a company's portfolio of business units. For acquisition decision making, the candidate firm might achieve "fit" with the acquiror's other business divisions through several means, for example, by taking advantage of production or marketing synergies.

In light of these conflicting theories, this research was designed to test the use of the CAPM through the simulation of acquisition decisions. The sample was a group of practicing corporate planners, namely, members of the North American Society for Corporate Planning, Inc. (NASCP). The methodology employed was one of policy capturing, which models strategic decision making through the use of a decision making exercise.

An othogonally designed simulation was built around the specific cues of the CAPM. The decision making exercise asked corporate planners to make acquisition decisions for 27 unique scenarios. A regression equation was then derived for each planner based on the acquisition decisions he or she made.

Based on the results of this research, there is no evidence that corporate planners use the CAPM as a tool for acquisition decision making. Three of the four terms in the CAPM were found to be significant in the decision making process, with the relative weights placed on the three cues being heavily skewed toward the rate of return of the proposed acquisition. In both the individual and group regressions, the weight placed on the correlation of returns between the acquisition candidate and the acquiror, even though significant, was quite small relative to the importance of rate of return. The planners appeared to be processing the cues of the CAPM as individual factors and not in conjunction with one another as an entire model.

These results support the findings of Slovic, Fischhoff, and Lichtenstein (1977) concerning the simplicity of decision making models. Additive linear models are capable of capturing a large percentage of the variance in human judgment; the interaction term of the CAPM added only one percentage point to the average individual R^2 value. Also, decision makers tend to rely on just a few criteria in processing information; evidence the group relative weight placed on the rate of return of the acquisition candidate in equation

(3.4)—93.0 of a possible 100 points. The candidates' rate of return was by far the controlling variable in the model.

Perhaps the model tested here is not appropriate for making acquisition decisions. For instance, several of the planners did not fill out the instrument, yet still took the time to write back with detailed comments on the selection of cues, along with their suggestions for improvement of the model. Indeed, 11 of the 22 respondents who wrote comments indicated that acquisitions should be "related." None suggested that acquisitions should be unrelated.

In conclusion, the use of the CAPM as a strategic planning tool as proposed by Naylor and Tapon (1982) takes too much liberty with the intended use of the model. In a strategic planning atmosphere, the model needs some major modifications in order to be useful. These modifications are discussed further in the next two chapters. The precepts of the CAPM represent a logical starting point for building an acquisition decision making model, but other qualitative factors certainly need to be considered, as evidenced by this study of practicing corporate planners.

REFERENCES

Bettis, Richard A. "Modern Financial Theory, Corporate Strategy, and Public Policy: Three Conundrums." *Academy of Management Review*, 1983, 8(3), 406–415.

Boardman, A. E., and Carruthers, N. E. "A Note on the Use of the CAPM as a Strategic Planning Tool." *Management Science*, 1985, 31, 1589–1592.

Brownlee, B. J. "Erratum to 'The Capital Asset Pricing Model: An Evaluation of Its Potential as a Strategic Planning Tool' by Thomas H. Naylor and Francis Tapon." *Management Science*, 1985, 29, 633.

Hoffman, P. F. "The Paramorphic Representation of Clinical Judgment." *Psychological Bulletin*, 1960, 57(2), 116–32.

Lintner, John. "The Valuation of Risk Assets and the Selection of Risky Investments in Stock Portfolios and Capital Budgets." *Review of Economics and Statistics*, 1965a, 47, 13–37.

Markowitz, Harry M. *Portfolio Selection: Efficient Diversification of Investments.* New York: John Wiley & Sons, 1959.

Modigliani, Franco, and Miller, Merton. "The Cost of Capital, Corporate Finance and the Theory of Investment." *American Economic Review*, 1958, 48(3), 261–297.

Mullins, David W., Jr. "Does the Capital Asset Pricing Model Work?" *Harvard Business Review*, 1982, 60, 105–114.

Naylor, Thomas H. "Reply to Brownlee Erratum." *Management Science*, 1983, 29, 633.

Naylor, Thomas H., and Tapon, Francis. "The Capital Asset Pricing Model: An Evaluation of Its Potential as a Strategic Planning Tool." *Management Science*, 1982, 28(10), 1166–1173.

North American Society for Corporate Planning. Membership Demographic Information, 1984 Information Package.

Porter, Michael E. *Competitive Strategy*. New York: The Free Press, 1980.

Salter, Malcolm S., and Weinhold, Wolf A. "Diversification via Acquisition: Creating Value." *Harvard Business Review*, 1978, 56, 166–176.

Sharpe, William F. "Capital Asset Prices: A Theory of Market Equilibrium Under Conditions of Risk." *Journal of Finance*, 1964, 19, 425–442.

Slovic, P., Fischhoff, B., and Lichtenstein, S. "Behavioral Decision Theory." *Annual Review of Psychology*, 1977, 28, 1–39.

Slovic, P., and Lichtenstein, S. "Comparison of Bayesian and Regression Approaches to the Study of Information Processing in Judgement." *Organizational Behavior and Human Performance*, 1971, 6, 649–744.

Stahl, Michael J., and Harrell, Adrian M. "The Evolution and Validation of a Behavioral Decision Theory Measurement Approach to Achievement, Power and Affiliation." *Journal of Applied Psychology*, 1982, 67(6), 744–751.

Stahl, M. J., and Zimmerer, T. W. "Modeling Strategic Acquisition Decisions." *Academy of Management Journal*, 1984, 27, 369–383.

Thompson, Arthur A., Jr., and Strickland, A. J., III. *Strategy and Policy: Concepts and Cases*. Plano, Tex.: Business Publications, 1981.

Tobin, James. "Liquidity Preference as Behavior Toward Risk." *Review of Economic Studies*, 1958, 25(2), 65–85.

Ward, J. "Comments on 'The Paramorphic Representation of Clinical Judgement'." *Psychological Bulletin*, 1962, 59, 74–76.

CHAPTER 4

Divestiture, Financial Diversification and the Capital Asset Pricing Model

DIVESTITURE AND CAPM

The recent trend in corporate divestiture represents a remarkable turn-around from the period of the 1960s when it was thought that acquisitions were the key to the continued success of the firm. While a significan amount of research and attention has been given to the strategic option of acquisition, very little light has been shed on the alternate issue of divestiture. This situation seems to stem from the perception that a divestment represents a failure on the part of the management team involved (Hayes, 1982; Alder, 1981). Consequently, prior to the early 1970s, few divestments took place and the executives who were involved were somewhat reluctant to discuss their parts in the decision process (Hayes, 1982; Lynch, 1980).

As firms have begun to reevaluate the divestment process and its impact on the company's overall performance (particularly its impact on stock prices), more divestments have taken place. Thus, it is reasonable to consider the act of divestment as a management tool that will be used more frequently in the future.

Hayes (1982) suggested that many managers see divestiture as simply the reverse side of the acquisition coin. Indeed, from a financial point of view, Boudreaux stated: "As an alteration of the firm's productive asset portfolio, divestiture is the mirror-image of asset acquisition or merger" (1975, p. 619). The key to this statement is based on the term "productive assets." Under these conditions, a divestiture is simply the reverse of acquisition in that a portion of the firm's assets are deleted rather than added. However, when considered from a corporate strategy perspective, Hayes (1982) pointed out that divestiture is quite different and thus decisions regarding

This chapter was written by Richard T. Christoph of James Madison University, Harrisonburg, Virginia, and Michael J. Stahl. An earlier version of this chapter was presented at the 1985 National Decision Sciences Institute meeting in Las Vegas and published in the *Proceedings*, pp. 689–91.

the act of divestiture must be made in that light. Specifically, the manager cannot simply take acquisition decision processes and do the reverse to accommodate the divestiture (Alder, 1981; Cohen and Slater, 1983; Donaldson, 1984).

A fundamental reason for a divestment is that it represents an attempt by the divesting firm to clarify its image as perceived by the stock market. Robert Bennett, Jr., assistant treasurer for the conglomerately diversified R. J. Reynolds Corporation, noted: "I don't know one analyst that follows the company as a conglomerate" (1984, p. 37). In this case as in others, potential investors cannot fully value the conglomerate firm's many, diverse business units. That is, the firm's overall strategy and resulting direction are unclear to the stock buyer. Brooks (1984) noted that as a direct result, the stock price of the conglomerate firm is priced artificially low. Seely suggested: "Investors prefer companies that are easy to understand and are willing to pay for them." (1981, p. 242) Slater (1984) suggested that the investor perform any diversification of a portfolio *not* the company. In this way, the investor can understand each business as it relates to his or her private portfolio. This entire concept was summarized by Weinger who stated: "The thicker the annual report, the lower the price earnings multiples" (1980, p. 55). Indeed, a number of financial researchers have noted the tendency for share prices to rise after a divestiture announcement (Hearth and Zaima, 1984; Jain, 1985; Miles and Rosenfeld, 1983; Rosenfeld, 1984; Zaima and Hearth, 1985).

These views differ markedly from the position postulated by Naylor and Tapon (1982). In their article "The Capital Asset Pricing Model: An Evaluation of Its Potential as a Strategic Planning Tool," the authors suggested that the management team of a firm will act like the holder of a portfolio of stocks and attempt to maximize returns subject to some risk factor. This model was developed by Sharpe (1964) and Lintner (1965) to assist the individual securities investor in building a portfolio under conditions of risk.

The CAPM model presented by Naylor and Tapon is contained in equation (3.2). This model is operationally tested in this study through the use of a decision modeling instrument. The construction of an instrument to test the CAPM centers around the concept of the model as presented by Naylor and Tapon in (3.2). They suggested that there are three areas that can and should be controlled by management: "In summary, in building a portfolio of businesses, a company should strive for high returns R_j in each business, low variances σ_j, and values of r_{jm} that are close to zero or negative"(p. 1170).

Therefore, in a divestment setting, the manager should seek to divest those business units in which low returns are expected, high variability is forecast, and that have *positive* return patterns related to other units that comprise the firm. It is this third notion that is most noteworthy from a strategic point of view.

Four distinct hypotheses dealing with divestiture and the CAPM were developed and tested. These hypotheses can be summarized as follows:

H1: Divestiture decisions follow the dictates provided by the Capital Asset Pricing Model as described by Naylor and Tapon (1982).

H2: There is a significant two-way interaction, shown in the CAPM, between r_{jm} and σ_j.

H3: All relative weights placed on the three decision cues by respondents are equal as was suggested by Naylor and Tapon (1982).

H4: There is no difference in the manager's propensity to divest a strategic business unit based on the new position of the manager's predecessor (either still with the firm or no longer with the firm).

H1 tests the suggestion made by Naylor and Tapon (1982) that the Capital Asset Pricing Model is useful to corporate managers who seek to reduce risk through the diversification of their portfolio of strategic business units.

The second hypothesis considers the effect of the two-way interaction that Naylor and Tapon (1982) suggest in their description of the CAPM between r_{jm} and σ_j. There is no conclusive evidence that managers do or do not use this interaction in reaching a decision. Hence, the question of the interaction versus the more common additive linear model is explained.

Hypothesis H3 extends hypothesis H1 and tests the concept of which variable component of the CAPM, if any, carries the most weight when the decision maker reaches a decision concerning divestment. Based on the evidence suggested by Naylor and Tapon (1982), it would seem that the three cues suggested by the model will influence the manager equally in a decision process.

The final hypothesis examines the possibility that power might influence the making of a divestment decision. It is possible that an executive may view a divestment decision as a means of solidifying his or her base of power in the organization. Certainly, this would depend on the current position of the executive's predecessor. For example, if that person was promoted, say to the board of directors, it may be that the new manager would avoid divesting the strategic business unit supported by the manager who is now his or her boss. Similarly, the opposite actions might occur if the original manager had left the firm for an outside position.

METHODOLOGY

The Divestiture/CAPM Decision Modeling Exercise

Rappaport suggested that previous capital budgeting questionnaires may suffer from a lack of statistical rigor in analysis. "Unfortunately, typical research design has emphasized gathering large quantities of information rather than making statistically valid inferences. Further, I would argue that insufficient attention was given to known design and interpretation difficulties associated with questionnaire surveys" (1979, p. 100). Ross (1978) noted the lack of robust tests of the theory. Markowitz (1983) reviewed several of the more recent tests and noted problems in testing the CAPM.

To avoid these potential pitfalls, this paper utilizes the decision modeling approach to strategic decisions that was develped by Stahl and Zimmerer (1984). These authors have proven the techniques's viability in the setting of corporate policy through the testing and capturing of decision processes on acquisitions. Such a method provides significant advantages over conventional questionnaire surveys such as giving the researcher the ability to test specific hypotheses that might be of interest. This is done by constructing the decision modeling instrument around "mini" scenarios in which a decision maker is asked to indicate how strongly he or she would divest a business unit based on certain cues presented. Further, by controlling these cues, the researcher can provide for a statistically rigorous, controlled experiment. Stahl (1986), Stahl and Harrell (1982), and Stahl and Zimmerer (1984) provide a complete description of this methodology.

To test the Capital Asset Pricing Model, a series of decisions was developed concerning a potential business unit which an executive might choose to divest. The executive was asked to rate how strongly he or she would support a divestment of the business unit described by the instrument. With each of the three CAPM cues at two levels, a $2 \times 2 \times 2$ design was chosen which yielded eight distinct business units. The first cue in the decision exercise is derived from the rate of return (expected profits) concept presented above. The second cue is based on the variability of the rate of return for the business unit. Finally, the third cue is based on the concept of business unit returns being correlated with that of the company as a whole.

The second decision the executive was asked to make was Decision B. It was included to investigate the potential that a divestment decision was seen as a management option to consolidate a base of power. Decision B is not directly associated with the Capital Asset Pricing Model and therefore is not included as part of the first decision. The additional information was listed at two possible ends—either the business unit was acquired by the former or the current president of the firm. Therefore, a double replicate of Decision A yielded a total of 16 hypothetical divestiture scenarios ($2 \times 2 \times 2 \times 2$).

An example from the actual decision modeling instrument is shown in Figure 4.1.

The Sampled Corporate Planners

It is highly likely that divestment decisions will be made by more than one person. Indeed, it is probable that an executive will call upon staff members who specialize in acquisition and divestment activities. For this reason, this

Figure 4.1
Sample Business Unit

**** Business Unit 1 ****

In this business unit, the following characteristics are present:

    ----the RATE OF RETURN in this business unit is.........LOW

    ----the VARIABILITY of the rate of return is...........LOW

    ----the CORRELATION between this unit's rate of return

        and the company's overall rate of return is....NEGATIVE

DECISION A: WITH THESE THREE FACTORS IN MIND, indicate the

            chance you would recommend divesting this business

            unit.

CHANCE OF

RECOMMENDING 0% 10% 20% 30% 40% 50% 60% 70% 80% 90% 100%

DIVESTITURE

FURTHER INFORMATION ABOUT BUSINESS UNIT 1: This business unit

    was acquired by the FORMER President of your firm.

DECISION B: With all of the above information in mind, indicate

       the chance you would recommend divesting this business

       unit.

CHANCE OF

RECOMMENDING 0% 10% 20% 30% 40% 50% 60% 70% 80% 90% 100%

DIVESTITURE

---

instrument was mailed to 1,498 members selected at random from the active membership of the North American Society for Corporate Planning, Inc. (NASCP). This sample did not overlap with the sample used in Chapter 3. This professional organization is made up of some 6,000 United States members who are "in a senior-level management position in a large, multinational firm interested in keeping abreast of new corporate planning techniques and applications" (NASCP, 1984).

Some 60 percent of the membership, according to membership demographics, design and administer their firm's strategic plans. This indicates that these decision makers are actively involved in the formulation and execution of actual strategic plans and would likely be involved in any divestment action of the firm. This figure was reflected in the responses to the survey in which some 213 (out of 343 or 62 percent) of the respondents indicated that they had been directly involved with a prior divestment decision. Therefore, the sample appeared to be representative of divestiture decision makers.

Each participant in the study received a packet of information which contained a personalized letter explaining the purpose of the study, the decision modeling instrument, and a prepaid return-mail envelope. This extra effort was undertaken to ensure the best possible response rate (Zikmund, 1984, p. 161). In a further effort to increase the response rate, the researchers offered feedback on the decisions made by the executive that could be compared with the decisions that were made by peers. A total of 212 individuals indicated they wanted feedback.

Data Analysis

Upon collection, the data were analyzed by a methodology similar to that of Stahl and Harrell (1982) and Stahl and Zimmerer (1984) who used a multiple regression model for each respondent. Before actually computing the model values, a squared multiple correlation coefficient (R^2) value is calculated on the responses within a given, complete instrument. Any instrument with statistically insignificant R^2 values was discarded as this indicated inconsistent internal decision making by the respondent (Stahl and Harrell, 1982).

Three independent variables are used; one for each of the cues for the Capital Asset Pricing Model decision making instrument. The dependent variable is the value given for the strength of the divestment decision made by the respondent. This model appears as equation (4.1).

$$Y_j = B_1(X_{1j}) + B_2(X_{2j}) + B_3(X_{3j}) + B_4(X_{2j}X_{3j}) \qquad (4.1)$$
$$j = 1,2, \ldots ,16$$

Where

Y_j = % chance of recommending divestiture for business unit j (Decision A);

B_1 = standardized regression coefficient or importance attributed to rate of return;

X_{1j} = rate of return for business unit j;

B_2 = standardized regression coefficient or importance attributed to variability of return;

X_{2j} = variability of business unit j's rate of return;

B_3 = standardized regression coefficient or importance attributed to correlation between business unit's rate of return and the company's overall rate of return;

X_{3j} = correlation of business unit j's rate of return and the company's overall rate of return;

B_4 = standardized regression coefficient or importance attributed to interaction between X_2 and X_3.

This formula also incorporates the interaction suggested by Naylor and Tapon (1982) between the variability of the returns and the correlation of the business unit's return with the firm as a whole. This correlation is seen as the level of strategic fit between the firm and the business unit in question.

This study also examined the possibility that only the main factors of the CAPM model (excluding the interaction term) were used by executives in reaching the divestment decision. This model, using the same variable definitions as equation (4.1), is shown in equation (4.2).

Equations (4.1) and (4.2) are similar to equations (3.3) and (3.4) respectively, with a few exceptions: (1) divestiture decisions, not acquisition decisions, are modeled here; (2) there are 16 decisions here, versus 27 in (3.3) and (3.4); (3) business units already in the firm are used here, versus external acquisition candidates.

$$Y_j = B_1(X_{1j}) + B_2(X_{2j}) + B_3(X_{3j}) \tag{4.2}$$

Duhaime and Schwenk (1985) suggest that executives are not likely to effectively process all information required for a divestment decision on a simultaneous basis and so will tend to simplify the decision and look only at a few major variables. By examining the additive model described in equation (4.2), in addition to the more complex interactive model in (4.1), it is possible to determine if the main variables in the CAPM are the focal points of executive decision making simplification.

RESULTS

A total of 405 instruments were returned by corporate executives of which 343 completed, usable instruments were included, representing a total of 5,488 divestment decisions made by strategic planning executives.

Each of the completed instruments was then evaluated on the respondent's consistency of decision making within the instrument using the R^2 methodology described earlier. The average R^2 was 0.87 which indicates that the executives were quite consistent in their decision making behavior. A high R^2 value indicates that the respondent was consistent in making decisions while a low value signifies inconsistency. Four instruments were discarded on this basis, each having an R^2 below .45 which corresponds to the 5 percent level of significance. Using the regression model described in equation (4.1), it was found that virtually all respondents (326/339) considered X_1 or the rate of return to be a significant factor in making a

Table 4.1
Individual Results for Equation (4.1) for Divestiture

Cue	Significant* Responses	% of 339
Rate of return (X1)	326	96
Variability of return (X2)	127	37
Correlation of returns (X3)	93	27
Interaction between X2 and X3	27	8
Full CAPM model (all four cues)	11	3

*p < .05.

Note: n = 339.

divestment decision. Indeed, 96 percent of these respondents looked upon a high rate of return as a strong reason not to divest the firm. See Table 4.1.

These returns were also examined for responses that considered only rate of return to be significant. A total of 145 individuals reached divestment decisions based *only* on this cue. This finding may support the conjecture by some that American managers tend to focus on returns to the exclusion of other factors.

In addition to the individual regressions, an overall regression incorporating 5,424 decisions (from instruments not dropped due to a low R^2 value) and equation (4.1) was calculated. This overall regression of all responseś also showed X_1 to be highly significant (p < .05) and have a large, negative standard estimate indicating that respondents would not consider divestment when returns are high. See Table 4.2.

Factor X_2, which represents the variability of the return, was found to be significant (p < .05) in Table 4.1 for 127 of the 339 respondents, or about 37 percent of the sample. This relationship proved true in the overall regression as well, with this factor being significant (p < .05) and positive in its standard estimate. This showed a readiness to divest those units which exhibit a high variability of returns.

Factor X_3 represents the correlation between the business unit and the parent firm. This factor proved significant for 93 respondents.

Tables 4.1 and 4.2 illustrate these relationships. In the overall regression, X_3 did not reach statistical significance. Hypothesis 1 was tested according to

Table 4.2
Group Regression Results for Equation (4.1) for Divestiture

Cue	Standardized Estimate	t score
Rate of return (X1)	-.783	-97.74*
Variability of return (X2)	.150	13.14*
Correlation of returns (X3)	-.017	-1.39
Interaction between X2 and X3	.006	0.50

*p < .05.

Note: n = 5,424.

the definition given by Naylor and Tapon (1982) who suggested that all three of the above factors and the interaction between X_2 and X_3 are considered when a divestment decision is made. When the data were examined from this perspective, only 11 individuals were found to have significant coefficients associated with all the variables and the interaction (p < .05). This represents a proportion of the sample of 3 percent and indicates that the decision makers were not following the dictates of the CAPM. Instead, they were considering specific, individual cues.

Hypothesis 1 was also examined using overall group regression results based on equation (4.1). Only two variables reached significance at the 5 percent level as shown in Table 4.2 which contains the group regression results.

Hypothesis 2, concerning the interaction between factor X_2 and X_3, appears not to be supported. Only 27 decision makers considered this interaction when making their decisions. As noted above, only 11 of these used the interaction in the setting described by the CAPM. The overall regression (Table 4.2) found this interaction to be insignificant at the p < .05 level.

Since the interaction was not significant, an overall regression analysis was re-run with only factors X_1, X_2, and X_3 per equation (4.2). Calculation of relative weights as suggested by Hoffman (1960) and Ward (1962) (equation 1.2) yielded the percentages of explained variation depicted in Table 4.3.

The cue for rate of return accounted for over 96 percent of all variation in the model. Clearly, this variable overshadowed all others in a divestment decision and indicated that the premise that all three cues carry the same weight in a divestment decision is not valid.

Table 4.3
Group Regression Results for Equation (4.2) for Divestiture

Cue	Relative Weight
Rate of return (X1)	96.3
Variability of return (X2)	3.6
Correlation of returns (X3)	0.1
TOTAL	100.0

Note: n = 5,424.

This is further supported by the information in Table 4.4. This information is based on the mean values for individual relative weights. All three main cues were found to be significant at the $p < .05$ level. However, R_j was again found to be by far the most important with a mean relative weight of 81.7 percent. Thus, the mean relative weights for equation (4.2) provide strong evidence that the weights placed on the cues by the decision makers were not the same.

Hypothesis 4 was tested through the use of a paired difference test on the two decisions (A and B) made by an individual respondent. The test was run on the difference between Decision A and Decision B. The resulting mean difference and t score appear in Table 4.5.

Table 4.4
Individual Relative Weights for Equation (4.2) for Divestiture

Cue	Mean Relative Weight
Rate of return (X1)	81.7
Variability of return (X2)	9.7
Correlation of returns (X3)	8.6
TOTAL	100.0

Note: n = 339.

Table 4.5
Paired Difference Test of Decision A—Decision B

Variable	Mean	t score
Difference	-.205	-16.76*

*p < .05

Note: n = 5,424.

There is a significant difference between paired responses for Decision A and Decision B. Therefore, the fourth hypothesis is rejected. It is concluded that there is a difference in a manager's propensity to divest a business unit based on the presence or absence of the manager who originally acquired it.

CONCLUSIONS

This research yielded empirical results concerning the use of the CAPM by actual managers who work in corporations. The results show that the CAPM was not used by these managers in making divestment decisions concerning autonomous business units. Interestingly, one responding manager noted that the firm's job is not to diversify. Rather, the shareholder will diversify risk and, in order to accurately assess the proper position of the firm in question, must be able to fully understand it. Therefore, the CAPM should be used by the shareholder (as it was initially designed to do) and the firm should provide a clear picture of the business it is in to enable the shareholder to balance his or her portfolio. Firms that do not provide this clarity of purpose may find that their share price is therefore undervalued. Further, a very large number of respondents indicated that only rate of return was considered when making a divestment decision. This may indicate that American management has become preoccupied with short-term returns.

Based on these findings, it is possible to suggest a number of potential revisions to the CAPM. Perhaps the most obvious of these would be to drop the interaction term from the model entirely. Certainly, based on this research, little insight is gained with its use. Second, it may be helpful to revise the CAPM concept to include other factors that would address the comment made by several respondents that the model was too simple. Since several comments were received concerning the strategic fit of a business unit to the parent firm (Thompson and Strickland, 1981), it may be reasonable to include components of fit in a proposed new divestment model. Two factors, marketing fit and production fit, are certainly major considerations in the determination of how well a business unit works with the rest of the firm. Further, it is possible to investigate these factors, to at least some extent, through the use of published data such as Standard Industrial Classification codes and similar sources.

Several studies from the financial and strategic management literature lend support to the notion that r_{jm} is not important. Stiglitz (1976) showed that under a fairly general set of conditions, the financial policy of the firm does not have an effect on the valuation of the firm. Donaldson (1984) deviated from standard concepts of financial theory when he wrote of the importance of fit between the proposed investment and the company's established business mission, perceived organizational strengths and managerial preferences. Rumelt (1979) noted that the highest levels of profitability were exhibited by those firms that were relatedly diversified, and that the lowest levels of profitability were associated with unrelated diversification. In an intensive analysis of PIMS-based data, Hambrick, Macmillan and Day (1982) noted that profitability was a function of the fundamental economic posture of the business: capital intensity, value added and manufacturing costs. The results also indicated that all four types of business in the Boston Consulting Group Portfolio Matrix were affected about equally. Therefore, there is no need to combine firms with different profitability histories as the CAPM's r_{jm} term implies. In an earlier analysis of PIMS data, Schoeffler, Buzzell, and Heany (1974) presented mixed results as they noted the highest levels of ROI for highly diversified and non-diversified firms and lower ROI for average diversification. Hamermesh and White (1984) presented data indicating that top management involvement with the management of subsidiary firms was associated with higher profitability. This runs counter to the CAPM dictates of structuring a firm solely with financial criteria in mind and little subsequent involvement by top management in the management of the firm. These studies question the importance of the r_{jm} term as proposed by the CAPM and suggest that marketing fit and production fit may be more fruitful areas for further research.

The proposed model is shown as equation (4.3).

$$V_j = R_j - \sigma_j + MF_j + PF_j \qquad \qquad (4.3)$$

Where

V_j = expected value of business unit j;

R_j = expected profit for business unit j;

σ_j = variability for R_j;

MF_j = marketing fit with the other business units;

PF_j = production fit with the other business units.

Two factors present in the CAPM are incorporated into this proposed model due to their significance in this study and the results of Chapter 3.

The additive model suggested as the more complex interactive model was not found to be utilized.

MF$_j$ and PF$_j$ could be based on actual or estimated costs or benefits that the overall firm derives from the inclusion of business j in its portfolio. Costs (or a lack of fit) would be negative and thus discourage the business unit's inclusion unless its returns were very high. Further, it is possible to incorporate other factors into such a model such as managerial competence, future strategic goals of the firm and the like.

Earlier suggestions that divestment may depend in part on the presence of the acquiring manager were borne out. It would seem that there is an emotional or political attachment to a business unit that may have a significant influence over its future. While this effect has been postulated by others, this is the first time known to the authors that empirical evidence based upon a large sample is available to support it. It is also interesting to note that one manager commented that this was the most important variable in the study. However, he mentioned that he was very careful not to let its influence show when completing the instrument.

The single most important conclusion of this study is that the CAPM was not used by these managers in making divestment decisions. Unrelated diversification was not supported by their 5,424 decisions.

REFERENCES

Alder, Herbert S. "The Thorough Way to Approach Divestment." *Management Focus*, May-June 1981, 3-7.

Bennett, Robert, Jr., quoted in "Some Concerns Find That the Push to Diversify Was a Costly Mistake." *Wall Street Journal*, 2 October 1984, p. 37.

Boudreaux, Kenneth J. "Divestiture and Share Price." *Journal of Financial and Quantitative Analysis*, November 1975, 619-26.

Brooks, Geraldine. "Some Concerns Find That the Push to Diversify Was a Costly Mistake." *Wall Street Journal*, 2 October 1984, p. 37.

Cohen, R., and Slatter, Stuart. "How to Divest." *Management Today*, May 1983, 92-95 and 133-136.

Donaldson, Gordon. "Financial Goals and Strategic Consequences." *Harvard Business Review*, May-June 1985, 57-66.

Donaldson, Gordon. *Managing Corporate Wealth: The Operation of a Comprehensive Financial Goals System*, New York: Praeger Publishers, 1984.

Duhaime, Irene M., and Schwenk, Charles R. "Consequences on Cognitive Simplification in Acquisition and Divestment Decision Making." *Academy of Business Management Review*, 1985, 10, 287-95.

Hambrick, D. C., Macmillan, I. C., and Day, D. L., "Strategic Attributes and Performance in the BCG Matrix—A PIMS-Based Analysis of Industrial Product Businesses." *Academy of Management Journal*, September 1982, 510-31.

Hamermesh, R. G., and White, R. E. "Manage Beyond Portfolio Analysis." *Harvard Business Review*, January-February 1984, 103-09.

Hayes, Robert. "New Emphasis on Divestment Opportunities." *Harvard Business Review*, July-August 1982.

Hearth, D. P., and Zaima, J. K. "Voluntary Divestitures and Value." *Financial Management*, Spring 1984, 10–16.

Hoffman, P. J. "The Paramorphic Representation of Clinical Judgment." *Psychological Bulletin*, 1960, (2) 111–132.

Jain, P. C. "The Effect of Voluntary Selloff Announcements on Shareholder Wealth." *Journal of Finance*, March 1985, 209–224.

Kollat, David T., Blackwell, Roger D., and Roberson, James F. *Strategic Marketing*. New York: Holt, Rinehart & Winston, 1972, 23–24.

Lintner, John. "The Valuation of Risk Assets and the Selection of Risky Investments in Stock Portfolios and Capital Budgets." *The Review of Economics and Statistics*, 1965, 47, 13–37.

Lynch, Mitchell. "Many Firms are Selling Off Acquisitions to Clarify Their Images, Lift Their Stocks." *Wall Street Journal*, 4 December 1980, 54.

Markowitz, N. "Nonnegative or Not Negative: A Question About CAPMs." *Journal of Finance*, May 1983, 283–295.

Miles, J. A., and Rosenfeld, J. D. "The Effect of Spinoff Announcements on Shareholder Wealth." *Journal of Finance*, December 1983, 1597–1606.

Mullins, R. H. "Does the Capital Asset Pricing Model Work?" *Harvard Business Review*, February 1982.

Macmillan, I. C., Hambrick, D. C., and Day, D. L. "The Product Portfolio and Profitability—A PIMS-Based Analysis of Industrial-Product Businesses." *Academy of Management Journal*, 1982, 25 (4), 733–755.

Naylor, T. H., and Tapon, R. "The Capital Asset Pricing Model: An Evaluation of Its Potential as a Strategic Planning Tool." *Management Science*, 1982, 28, 1166–1173.

Nees, Danielle. "Increase Your Divestment Effectiveness." *Strategic Management Journal*, 1981, 2, 119–130.

North American Society for Corporate Planning. Membership Demographic Information. 1984 Information Package.

Rappaport, Allen. "A Critique of Capital Budgeting Questionnaires." *Interfaces*, May 1979, 100–102.

Rosenfeld, J. D. "Additional Evidence on the Relation Between Divestiture Announcements and Shareholder Wealth." *Journal of Finance*, December 1984, 1437–1448.

Ross, S. A. "The Current Status of the Capital Asset Pricing Model." *Journal of Finance*, 1978, 33, 885–901.

Rumelt, R. P. "Diversification Strategy and Profitability." *Strategic Management Journal*, 1979, 3 (4), 359–369.

Schoeffler, S., Buzzell, R. D., and Heany, D. G. "Impact of Strategic Planning on Profit Performance." *Harvard Business Review*, March-April 1974, 137–145.

Seely, Michael, quoted in Greenbaum, Mary, "Making The Most of Unnoticed Assets." *Fortune*, 15 June 1981, pp. 241–242.

Sharpe, William F. "Capital Asset Prices: A Theory of Market Equilibrium under Conditions of Risk." *Journal of Finance*, 1964, 19, 425–442.

Shirley, R. C. "Limiting the Scope of Strategy: A Decision-Based Approach." *Academy of Management Review*, 1982, 7, 262–268.

Slater, Malcolm, quoted in Brooks, Geraldine, "Some Concerns Find That the Push to Diversify Was a Costly Mistake." *Wall Street Journal*, 2 October 1984, p. 37.

Stahl, Michael J. *Managerial and Technical Motivation: Assessing Needs for Achievement, Power and Affiliation.* New York: Praeger Publishers, 1986.

Stahl, Michael J., and Harrell, Adrian M. "The Evolution and Validation of a Behavioral Decision Theory Measurement Approach to Achievement, Power and Affiliation." *Journal of Applied Psychology*, 1982, 67, 744-751.

Stahl, Michael J., and Zimmerer, Thomas W. "Modeling Strategic Acquisition Policies: A Simulation of Executives Acquisition Decisions." *Academy of Management Journal*, 1984, 27, 369-383.

Stiglitz, J. "On the Irrelevance of Corporate Financial Policy." In S. C. Myers, ed., *Modern Developments in Financial Management.* New York: Praeger Publishers, 1976, pp. 136-151.

Thompson, A. A., Jr., and Strickland, A. H. *Strategy and Policy: Concepts and Cases.* Rev. ed. Plano, Tex.: Business Publications, Inc., 1981.

Ward, J. "Comments on The Paramorphic Representation of Clinical Judgment." *Psychological Bulletin*, 1962, 59, 74-76.

Weinger, Norman, quoted in "Many Firms Are Selling Off Acquisitions To Clarify Their Images, Lift Their Stocks." *Wall Street Journal*, 4 December 1980, p. 54.

Zaima, J. K., and Hearth, D. P. "The Wealth Effects of Voluntary Selloffs: Implications for Divesting and Acquiring Firms." *Journal of Financial Research*, Fall 1985, 227-236.

Zikmund, William G. *Business Research Methods.* Chicago: The Dryden Press, 1984.

CHAPTER 5

Acquisition Decisions, Strategic Fit, Profitability and Risk

INTRODUCTION

Over the last three decades, a growing number of firms have incorporated diversification as an integral part of their corporate growth strategy (Rumelt, 1974). Not all diversification attempts have been successful, nor have diversifying firms shown similar patterns in the implementation of diversification strategies. Although many theoretical frameworks have been proposed and studied, the contradictory nature of empirical findings has left both researchers and practitioners without a concrete foundation for understanding diversification.

The acquisition fever of the sixties resulted in the birth of hundreds of conglomerates—firms that acquired businesses without regard to the relationships between the acquired businesses and their primary business. The incentives were purely financial, and most often managerial implications were overlooked (Drucker, 1976, 1981; Salter and Weinhold, 1978). Recent trends in acquisition-oriented diversification strategies indicate that diversification strategies are becoming more relatedly oriented—where a synergy can be achieved between different business units (Dobrzynski, 1988; Rumelt, 1974; Drucker, 1981). In spite of the recent trend, two different schools of thought continue to prevail. The advocates of financial portfolio theory justify conglomerate diversification, while proponents of strategic fit advocate related diversification. The purpose of this chapter is to integrate key variables of both schools and study their use by corporate planners in a decision making environment.

This chapter was written by Alok Srivastava of Georgia State University and Michael J. Stahl. An earlier version of this chapter was presented at the 1987 National Decision Sciences Institute meeting in Boston and published in the *Proceedings*, pp. 1169–71.

Diversification and Financial Portfolio Theory

The basic notion of portfolio theory in the context of corporate diversification is imbedded in the concept of investment risk reduction. Risk has been defined and operationalized as the variability of a firm's earnings stream (Modigliani and Miller, 1958; Bettis and Hall, 1982; Montgomery and Singh, 1982). The reasoning is that if the returns of two businesses are negatively correlated, the variability of the combination is smaller than the sum of each firm's variability in returns. Through an efficient selection of businesses, a firm can hence ensure a steady flow of earnings and thus increase its value (Naylor and Tapon, 1982).

The foundations of portfolio theory are represented by the Capital Asset Pricing Model (CAPM) (Chapters 3 and 4). Modigliani and Miller (1958) were the first to propose a risk component of the cost of capital. Markowitz (1959), by developing a model for portfolio selection, promoted the notion that risk is reflected in the variability of the earnings stream. Tobin (1958) associated risk with rate of return and proposed that investors would require a risk premium for investing in riskier securities. Through efficient portfolio selection, it is theoretically possible to eliminate risk (Markowitz, 1959; Tobin, 1958, Lintner, 1965). This concept of risk reduction through efficient portfolio selection gave birth to the idea of conglomerate diversification.

Lewellen (1971) proposed a financial rationale for conglomerate mergers. There are three main financial sources of gain possible through conglomerate mergers: transient errors in the market's evaluation of acquisition candidates, utilization of unused debt capacity of an acquired firm after acquisition, and diminished variability of total corporate earnings through portfolio diversification implied by conglomeration. Lewellen also argued that the concept of risk reduction is not sufficient to justify conglomerate diversification. He used the common argument that in an efficient market, as assumed by Lintner (1965) and Sharpe (1964), merging shares would already be included in individual portfolios in precisely merger proportions.

A number of potential applications of the CAPM for diversifying firms were outlined by Mullins (1982) and Naylor and Tapon (1982). Mullins (1982) argued that the CAPM can be used to discount the potential cash flow of the acquisition candidate. By selecting profitable firms with relatively lower cost of capital, it should be possible for the diversifying firm to increase its value. Naylor and Tapon (1982) advanced the idea that the CAPM can be a valuable tool in strategic planning. They forwarded a model for evaluating the value of a firm based on the precepts of the CAPM. Chapters 3 and 4 indicate that the CAPM is not used by exectutives in making either acquisition or divestiture decisions.

Financial portfolio theory considers only profitability and risk characteristics in evaluating firms for acquisition (Baron, 1979; Mullins,

1982; Naylor and Tapon, 1982). Such acquisition models are too simplistic and do not provide an adequate rationale for diversification (Chapters 3 and 4; Salter and Weinhold, 1978). By not considering strategic variables and managerial implications, financial portfolio theory seems to have serious limitations in its use to evaluate potential acquisition candidates.

Diversification and Strategic Fit

The theory of strategic management widely differs from that of financial portfolio theory in providing a rationale for diversification. The recommendations made by proponents of strategic management are diametrically opposite to those made by adherents of financial portfolio theory concerning diversification. Acquisition candidates are evaluated based on the degree of strategic fit with the acquiring firm's core business (Dobrzynski, 1988). Diversification strategies are meaningful only if logical relationships exist between the various business units of the firm (Ansoff, 1965; Drucker, 1976, 1981; Salter and Weinhold, 1978). These relationships are determined by the level of strategic fit that exists between the different business units.

Thompson and Strickland (1981) broadly classified strategic fit into three categories: product-market fit, operating fit, and management fit. Since managerial activities are viewed as a subset of operating and marketing fit, strategic fit can be broadly classified into marketing fit and operating fit. This classification is consistent with Rumelt's (1974) categorization of diversified firms. Marketing fit is the extent to which different products utilize common distribution channels, the same promotion techniques, and/or the same sales force and are bought by the same customers. Operating fit results from purchasing and warehousing economies, joint utilization of plant and equipment, overlaps in technology and engineering design, carry over of research and development activities, and/or common labor requirements. Firms that acquire businesses with a high degree of strategic fit are viewed as pursuing strategies of related diversification (Caldwell and Harrison, 1986; Drucker, 1976; Montgomery, 1982; Rumelt, 1974; Salter and Weinhold, 1978).

Although strategic fit has been addressed by several researchers, no consistent operationalization of this concept has resulted. Venkatraman and Cammilus (1984) provide an extensive review of research related to strategic fit. In the context of corporate diversification and acquisitions, several researchers have indirectly considered implications of strategic fit. Rumelt's (1974) categorical measure of diversity incorporates the concepts of both marketing fit and operating fit. This measure involves a certain degree of subjectivity (Pitts and Hopkins, 1984; Rumelt, 1974). This problem was overcome through the use of continuous measures (Caldwell and Harrison, 1986; Montgomery, 1982; Palepu, 1985).

Research Objective

The diversification literature is replete with contradictions regarding which strategy is superior. Due to the absence of a unifying theory, corporate planners do not have reliable tools to evaluate acquisition candidate firms. Most studies on acquisition decision making have been prescriptive in nature. Researchers have tried to develop normative models to describe how decision makers *ought* to evaluate various criteria in making acquisition-related decisions (Biggadike, 1979; Cameron, 1977; Drucker, 1976, 1981; Kumar, 1977; Salter and Weinhold, 1978). The principal objective of this descriptive study was to combine the key criteria outlined by both financial portfolio theory and strategic management, and to test their use by corporate planners in evaluating potential acquisition candidates.

As discussed above, financial theory considers only profitability and risk characteristics in evaluating businesses. Most of the determinants of related diversification, as argued above, can be appropriately summarized by marketing fit and operating fit. Rate of return was used as a measure of profitability; variance of the rate of return was used as a measure of risk (Bettis and Hall, 1982; Montgomery and Singh, 1982). Marketing fit and operating fit represented strategic fit variables in this study. The value of the acquisition candidate firm was hypothesized as a function of these variables. The decision making model tested is outlined by equation (5.1).

$$Y_j = B_1(X_{1j}) + B_2(X_{2j}) + B_3(X_{3j}) + B_4(X_{4j}) + B_{12}(X_{1j}*X_{2j})$$
$$+ B_{13}(X_{1j}*X_{3j}) + B_{14}(X_{1j}*X_{4j}) + B_{23}(X_{2j}*X_{3j}) + B_{24}(X_{2j}*X_{4j})$$
$$+ B_{34}(X_{3j}*X_{4j}) \tag{5.1}$$

Where

Y_j = perceived value of acquisition candidate j;

B_1 = standardized regression coefficient or importance attributed to rate of return (RR);

X_{1j} = RR of acquisition candidate j;

B_2 = standardized regression coefficient or importance attributed to variability of RR;

X_{2j} = variability of acquisition candidate j's RR;

B_3 = standardized regression coefficient or importance attributed to marketing fit;

X_{3j} = marketing fit of candidate firm j with acquiring firm;

B_4 = standardized regression coefficient or importance attributed to operating fit;

X_{4j} = operating fit of candidate firm j with acquiring firm.

Consistent with the decision-modeling literature, only two-way interaction terms were included in equation (5.1) (Stahl and Zimmerer, 1984). By developing such a model, the acquisition policies of a firm can easily be summarized. To determine which variables are the most important determinants of value, acquisition policies were related to firm performance. The performance variable used was the annual average price earnings (PE) ratio. This measure was chosen since it is a proxy measure of the value of a firm. The next objective was to determine if there were significant differences in the acquisition policies of firms in different categories, categorized by industry and size. Thus, the following hypotheses were tested:

H1: Corporate planners do not use rate of return, variability of rate of return, marketing fit, operating fit, and all two-way interactions of these cues, when evaluating firms for acquisition.

H2: None of the weights placed by corporate planners on the four cues are significantly related to their firm's performance.

H3: There is no significant difference between weights placed on the four different cues across different industries.

H4: There is no significant difference in the weights placed on various cues across firms of different size.

METHODOLOGY

The Acquisition/Strategic Fit Decision Making Exercise

The exercise was developed by generating 16 decision making scenarios. These decision making scenarios represented characteristics of 16 potential acquisition candidates. This study focused on four factors each at two levels (high and low), which results in the use of a $2 \times 2 \times 2 \times 2$ experimental design. Each respondent was asked to evaluate each acquisition candidates by placing his/her level of recommendation on a scale of -5 to $+5$. Respondents were requested to make evaluations consistent with the acquisition policies of their firms. The instrument also requested respondents to provide some financial information on the firm they represented. An example of the simulated acquisition candidate is presented in Figure 5.1.

The Sampled Corporate Planners

A total of 271 instruments were mailed to corporate executives involved in corporate planning who earlier had been part of the samples studied in Chapters 3 and 4. Each member of the sample was a member of the North American Society for Corporate Planning. Members of the sample received a package containing the instrument, a postage-paid return envelope, and a cover letter. The cover letter briefly described the exercise, and requested

Figure 5.1
Sample Acquisition Candidate

ACQUISITION CANDIDATE FIRM #1

The characteristics of this firm in the context of your firm are
outlined below. Please evaluate this firm for its possible
acquisition by your firm.

    The RATE OF RETURN of this firm is----------------------HIGH

    The VARIABILITY OF The RATE OF RETURN of this firm is----LOW

    The MARKETING FIT of this firm with your firm is--------HIGH

    The OPERATING FIT of this firm with your firm is--------HIGH

DECISION: Given the levels for the factors for this acquisition
candidate, indicate how strongly you would recommend its
acquisition.

```
Strongly                                              Strongly
Against     -5  -4  -3  -2  -1  0  +1  +2  +3  +4  +5       For
Acquisition                                           Acquisition
```

---

respondents to evaluate cases in the context of their firm. One hundred and
thirteen properly completed instruments were returned.

Data Analysis

The first set of analyses involved the development of decision making
models for each respondent using equation (5.1). The dependent variable Y_j
was the perceived value of the acquisition candidate which could take on
values between -5 and $+5$. All independent variables X_1 through X_4 could
take on two values each, $+1$(high) and -1(low) to preserve orthogonality.
Each model was tested for internal consistency.

Hypothesis 2 was tested by computing the correlation coefficients between each relative weight (equation 1.2) and the performance measure. To
test H3, firms were categorized by the industry of their principal business.
An industry group was used only if it was represented by at least five
respondents. The means of relative weights for each subsample were

subjected to a multivariate analysis of variance (MANOVA). H4 was tested by using firm size to generate subsamples. The mean relative weights of these subsamples were first subjected to MANOVA to test for overall differences and then to an analysis of variance to determine specific differences.

RESULTS

One hundred and thirteen properly completed instruments were received. All data were collected within six weeks after the mailout of instruments. Every participant provided decisions on each of the 16 cases. Decision making models for each decision maker were developed using equation (5.1). Tests for internal consistency revealed that only one respondent was not consistent in his/her evaluations. This response was dropped from the study resulting in the use of 112 responses. The average R^2 for models developed using equation (5.1) was an encouraging 0.92. One hundred and twelve instruments resulted in the use of 1,792 decisions. These decisions were used to develop decision making models using equation (5.1).

Hypothesis 1 was tested by performing a number of analyses. First, a group regression model based on equation (5.1) was developed using all 1,792 decisions. The results of the group regression analyses are presented in Table 5.1. All four main effects $(X_1—X_4)$ were significant at $p < .01$, while only two interaction terms $(X_1*X_2$ and $X_3*X_4)$ were significant. Table 5.1 also presents the relative weight associated with each term in equation (5.1).

As shown in Table 5.1, no single interaction effect had a relative weight greater than 1 percent. Moreover, the total relative weight for all interaction terms was 1.39 percent which meant that 98.71 percent of the decision making was attributed to main effects. A number of earlier studies found that additive main effects models explain most of the variance in decision making (Slovic, Fischhoff, and Lichtenstein, 1977).

Results of individual regression analyses, which are shown in Table 5.2, indicated that only a few participants processed information interactively. Based on these results in Tables 5.1 and 5.2, H1 was rejected.

Based on these results and those of earlier studies, it was decided to test an alternate decision making model with only main effects. This model is described by equation (5.2).

$$Y_j = B_1(X_{1j}) + B_2(X_{2j}) + B_3(X_{3j}) + B_4(X_{4j}) \tag{5.2}$$

To test this decision making model, hypothesis 1 was altered and a new hypothesis, H1', was tested.

H1': Corporate planners do not use rate of return, variability of rate of return, marketing fit, and operating fit, when evaluating candidate firms for acquisition.

All 1,792 decisions were pooled to develop a regression model based on equation (5.2). The results of this analysis are shown in Table 5.3. As expected from the results of Table 5.1, all main effects were significant at

Table 5.1
Group Regression Results Using Equation (5.1)

Cue	Relative Weight	t
Rate of Return (X_1)	40.20	38.31 *
Variability of RR (X_2)	3.65	-11.55 *
Marketing fit (X_3)	33.08	34.75 *
Operating fit (X_4)	21.64	28.11 *
X_1*X_2	0.93	-5.83 *
X_1*X_3	0.07	1.65
X_1*X_4	0.00	-0.06
X_2*X_3	0.01	-0.62
X_2*X_4	0.06	1.55
X_3*X_4	0.32	-3.47*

*$p < .01$.

Note: n = 1,792.

Table 5.2
Individual Results for Equation (5.1)

Cue	Significant* Responses	% of 112
Rate of return (X_1)	90	80.35
Variability of RR (X_2)	23	20.53
Marketing fit (X_3)	82	73.21
Operating fit (X_4)	66	58.92
X_1*X_2	6	5.35
X_1*X_3	4	3.57
X_1*X_4	5	4.46
X_2*X_3	0	0.00
X_2*X_4	1	0.08
X_3*X_4	5	4.46

* $p < .01$.

Note: n = 112.

Table 5.3
Group Regression Results for Equation (5.2)

Cue	Relative Weight	t
Rate of return (X_1)	40.81	37.83 *
Variability of RR (X_2)	3.70	-11.40 *
Marketing fit (X_3)	33.58	34.31 *
Operating fit (X_4)	21.97	27.76 *

* $p < .01$.

Note: n = 1,792.

$p < .01$. The reduction in R^2 due to the absence of the interaction terms was less than 1 percent, which implied that equation (5.2) was a superior and a simpler model of acquisition decision making. Moreover, by eliminating the interaction terms, more respondents had significant main effects (Table 5.4).

These results clearly reject H1'. It can be inferred that equation (5.2) adequately describes the decision making behavior of corporate planners when evaluating firms for acquisition. Profitability of candidates firms by far received the greatest importance. Both marketing fit and operating fit variables were significantly used by respondents in their evaluations. Risk received the lowest degree of importance. Variability of rate of return,

Table 5.4
Individual Responses for Equation (5.2)

Cue	Significant* Responses	% of 112	Mean Relative Weight
Rate of return (X_1)	100	89.28	38.70
Variability of RR (X_2)	28	25.00	7.85
Marketing fit (X_3)	92	82.14	31.40
Operating fit (X_4)	78	69.64	21.79

* $p < .01$

Note: n = 112.

Table 5.5
Correlations of Cues with Price Earnings Ratio

Cue	PE Ratio
Rate of return (X_1)	-.35 *
Variability of RR (X_2)	-.01
Marketing fit (X_3)	.32 *
Operating fit (X_4)	.10

*$p < .01$.

Note: $n = 62$.

which was defined as a measure of risk, had a negative standardized coefficient. This implied that corporate planners associated a low value to firms that had greater variability in their earnings. All other criteria had positive standardized coefficients. Based on the results presented in Tables 5.3 and 5.4, it was decided to use equation (5.2) in all subsequent analyses.

The purpose of testing H2 was to determine if different acquisition policies received different evaluations by the stock market. The average annual price earnings ratio for the most recent fiscal year was used because this measure directly reflects the market's evaluation of a firm's value. Only 62 respondents provided this information. This hypothesis is highly exploratory and is based on the assumption that respondents made decisions in accordance with the acquisition policies of their respective firms. Correlation coefficients of each relative weight with price earnings ratios were computed and tested for significance. Results of these analyses are shown in Table 5.5.

Two out of the four correlation coefficients were significant at the 1 percent level. It is interesting to note that firms that were emphasizing profitability in their acquisition policies were not highly rewarded by the stock market. A relatively higher weight on rate of return of the candidate firm directly implies a relatively lower weight on other variables especially the strategic fit variables. The stock market realizes that acquisition of profitable firms is a rare phenomenon and to receive a higher evaluation the firm must demonstrate degrees of strategic fit in their acquisition strategies. This argument is further supported by the positive significant correlation between the relative weight associated with marketing fit and price earnings ratio.

Both of the financial portfolio theory variables, profitability and risk, had a negative sign associated with their correlation coefficients. This suggests that the market does not place a high value on firms pursuing strategies of conglomerate diversification. Both strategic fit variables had a positive sign associated with the correlation coefficients, lending the market's support for related diversification. The correlation of PE with marketing fit was significant, while the correlation between PE and operating fit (X_4) was not. This finding is consistent with Kitching's (1967) supposition that marketing synergies were predictable and could be evaluated by the market, while operating synergies need a long time frame to materialize and are usually not explicit. These findings are also consistent with the propositions put forth by Drucker (1981) and Salter and Weinhold (1978).

The correlation coefficients were computed based on data provided by 62 respondents. Thirty-one of these respondents provided their respective firm's corporate name. For validation purposes, actual average price earnings ratio (PE1) of these firms were obtained from the Value Line Investment Survey. The correlation between reported PE and actual PE1 was 0.70 $(p < .01)$. This result adds validity to these findings.

Hypothesis 3 explored whether the acquisition policies were different for different industrial groupings. Industry information provided by respondents was used to generate various subsamples. For statistical considerations, it was decided to use only subsamples with five or more respondents. This constraint resulted in the use of seven industrial categories. A multivariate analysis of variance (MANOVA) was performed to test for significant differences in multivariate mean vectors of the relative weights across different industrial categories. The MANOVA F was 1.07 which was not significant at any meaningful level. The results of this analysis are shown in Table 5.6.

The results shown in Table 5.6 failed to reject hypothesis 3. This implies that decision makers were not influenced by the nature of their principal industry in evaluating potential acquisition candidates. There was general agreement among decision makers in terms of the relative importance placed on the four cues across all industrial groups. This finding reinforces our belief that general theories of acquisitions can be developed and used independent of specific industries as suggested in Chapter 2.

To test hypothesis 4, firms were classified into three categories based on the sales information provided by the respondents. Large firms were those that had annual sales greater than $1 billion; medium-sized firms had sales between $100 and $999 million; and, small firms had annual sales of less than $100 million. Vector means of relative weights were compared by performing MANOVA. The MANOVA F was 2.12, which was significant at $p < .10$, signifying overall differences in means across size categories. Next, four one-way analyses of variance (ANOVA) were performed to identify specific differences. Results of these analyses are tabulated in Table 5.7.

It is interesting to note that decision makers representing small firms associated the highest importance with the rate of return (X_1) of acquisition candidate firms, while decision makers representing large firms placed the least importance on this criteria. Small firms typically do not have a portfolio

Table 5.6
Comparison of Mean Relative Weights Across Industries

| Industry | n | Mean Relative Weight | | | |
		X_1	X_2	X_3	X_4
Banks and Holding Cos.	5	54.94	11.04	17.47	16.40
Chemicals	8	30.89	3.70	49.95	15.30
Conglomerates	9	37.44	9.01	28.09	25.22
Nonbank Financial	6	43.66	12.78	28.81	14.63
Service Industries	29	37.01	7.70	31.68	24.34
Misc. Manufacturing	5	43.67	5.88	23.82	26.49
Natural Resources (fuel)	7	48.23	2.61	27.39	21.65

Note: MANOVA F = 1.07, not significant.

Note: X_1 = rate of return (RR); X_2 = variability of RR; X_3 = marketing fit; X_4 = operating fit.

Table 5.7
Comparison of Mean Relative Weights Across Firm Size

| Size | n | Mean Relative Weight | | | |
		X_1	X_2	X_3	X_4
Large	39	31.25	6.70	35.76	25.61
Medium	31	39.64	11.39	30.25	18.55
Small	23	47.66	4.67	28.77	19.16
ANOVA F		4.34*	2.63*	1.10	2.25
MANOVA F				2.12*	

* $p < .10$.

Note: X_1 = rate of return (RR); X_2 = variability of RR; X_3 = marketing fit; X_4 = operating fit.

of businesses, and are usually single business firms. The main strategy is to ensure growth, and since they do not have sufficient resources to finance growth, acquisitions that will directly increase profitability are sought.

The means of variability of rate of return (X_2) were also significantly different for the three size categories. Decision makers representing medium-sized firms emphasized risk characteristics to a greater extent than did respondents in other categories. Medium-sized firms usually have some cash-generating businesses. Their strategies emphasize stabilization of earnings to ensure a steady growth (Chandler, 1962). Alternatively, large firms already have reliable cash-generating businesses and good control over their markets and do not need to emphasize direct risk reduction in their acquisitions. In other words, large firms can afford to seek long-term benefits in acquisitions rather than to emphasize short-term investment risk reduction.

There was no significant difference in the means of relative weight associated with marketing fit (X_3) or operating fit (X_4) across the three size categories. Corporate planners, irrespective of their firm size, placed statistically equal importance on marketing fit and operating fit in acquisitions. Although the difference was not significant, large firms placed the highest importance on these criteria compared to other firms. If the two strategic fit variables are combined, the average combined relative weight for the large firms (61.37) is significantly greater than the average combined relative weight of other size categories. Apparently, corporate planners of large firms emphasize strategic fit to a greater degree when evaluating candidate firms for acquisition.

CONCLUSIONS

The concept of "synergy" and the notions of strategic fit were introduced by Ansoff (1965). Although these propositions have been aired widely in the literature for over two decades, a good understanding of the dimensions of strategic fit in the context of acquisitions is lacking. Partly due to this lack, researchers have tried to propagate financial portfolio models as planning tools for corporate acquisitions (Baron, 1979; Naylor and Tapon, 1982). But experience and research are proving that the underlying assumptions of the portfolio models are too simplistic and cannot be directly extended to the arena of corporate diversification (Chapters 3 and 4; Salter and Weinhold, 1978). The problem of developing relevant models for acquisitions is further confounded by the unavailability of knowledge regarding the variables used by corporate planners in the successful implementation of acquisition strategies. By employing decision modeling techniques, we have demonstrated the relative importance corporate planners place on the various criteria considered in this study. This knowledge can be of valuable use to both corporate planners and researchers in their quest for developing a better understanding of the acquisition process.

An examination of the relative weights computed by both group and individual regressions revealed that corporate planners used all four criteria considered in this study. Profitability of acquisition candidates was the most important factor considered, but only marginally more important than marketing fit and operating fit. The risk factor represented by the variability of rate of return received the lowest relative importance. Strategic fit was probably perceived as a better means to manage risk, which explains the low relative importance placed on variability of return. These findings call for the development of quantifiable measures of marketing fit and operating fit.

When acquisition policies were related to a market performance variable, the price earnings ratio, two conclusions were evident. Consistent with Kitching's (1967) arguments, the stock market can identify marketing synergies and hence places a higher value on firms that emphasize marketing fit in their acquisitions. Operating synergies are less tangible and take a long time to materialize. On the other hand, firms that emphasized financial aspects rather than strategic aspects had lower price earnings ratios. These findings are consistent with propositions put forth by Salter and Weinhold (1978) and Drucker (1981). To receive a high evaluation by the stock market the acquiring firm must demonstrate what kind of marketing synergies it hopes to achieve in its acquisitions. Implications are that firms should concentrate on how their basic strengths can be transferred to the acquired businesses rather than concentrating on purely financial aspects (Montgomery, 1982; Rumelt, 1974).

There were no significant overall differences in the acquisition policies across various industrial categories. Corporate planners of firms in different industries were in general agreement about the relative importance placed on various criteria. Implications are that researchers can develop unifying and generalizable theories of corporate diversification (Baron, 1979; Dobrzynski, 1988; Naylor and Tapon 1982; Rumelt, 1974; Salter and Weinhold, 1978).

Corporate planners representing firms of different sizes did show significant differences in terms of relative importance placed on the four criteria. Large firms emphasized strategic fit variables more than other firms. Medium-sized firms also emphasized risk reduction through acquisitions to ensure steady growth. These implications are consistent with Chandler's (1962) identification of the stages of a firm's growth and Rumelt's finding that related diversification strategies resulted in superior performance. It appears that there is a need to consider size variables in future diversification-oriented studies.

There are limitations in using decision modeling to understand the strategy process. But the insight that can be gained can prove to be very valuable. One major limitation is that the methodology imposes a constraint on the number of variables that can be used in a study. This problem can be overcome by generating a hierarchy of variables and studying different parts of this hierarchy separately. Knowledge gained through such studies can provide researchers with opportunities to test new models with actual data. The insight gained can be of great importance in our quest to develop a better understanding of the strategic management process.

REFERENCES

Ansoff, H. *Corporate Strategy.* New York: McGraw-Hill, 1965.

Baron, D. "Investment Policy, Optimality, and Mean Variance Model." *Journal of Finance,* 1979, 207, 32.

Bettis, R. A., and Hall, W. K. "Diversification Strategy: Accounting Determined Risk and Accounting Determined Return." *Academy of Management Journal,* 1982, 25, (2), 254–264.

Biggadike, R. "The Risky Business of Diversification." *Harvard Business Review,* July-August 1979, 99–110.

Caldwell, L. G., and Harrison, J. S. "The Content of Corporate Level Strategy in Highly Diversified Firm." *Proceedings,* Decision Science Institute, Honolulu, 1986, pp. 1233–1235.

Cameron, D. "Appraising Companies for Acquisition." *Long Range Planning,* 1977, 10, 21–28.

Chandler, A. *Strategy and Structure.* Cambridge: The MIT Press, 1962.

Dobrzynski, J. "Learning from the Mangled Mergers of the Past." *Business Week,* 21 March 1988, 126.

Drucker, P. F. *Management.* New York: Harper and Row, 1976.

Drucker, P. F. "The Five Rules of Successful Acquisitions." *The Wall Street Journal,* October 15 1981.

Kitching, J. "Why Do Mergers Miscarry?" *Harvard Business Review,* 1967, 45(6), 84–101.

Kumar, P. "Corporate Growth Through Acquisitions." *Managerial Planning,* 1977, 39, 9–12.

Lewellen, W. G. "A Pure Financial Rationale for the Conglomerate Merger." *Journal of Finance,* May 1971, 521–537.

Lintner, J. "The Valuation of Risk Assets and the Selection of Risky Investments." *Review of Economics and Statistics,* 1965, 47, 13–37.

Markowitz, H. M. *Portfolio Selection: Efficient Diversification of Investments.* New York: John Wiley & Sons, 1959.

Modigliani, R. W., and Miller, M., "The Cost of Capital, Corporate Finance, and the Theory of Investment." *American Economic Review,* 1958, 48 (3), 261–297.

Montgomery, C. A. "The Measurement of Firm Diversification: Some New Empirical Evidence." *Academy of Management Journal,* 1982, 299–307.

Montgomery, C. A., and Singh, H. "Diversification Strategy and Systematic Risk." *Strategic Management Journal,* 1982, 181–191.

Mullins, D. W. "Does the Capital Asset Pricing Model Work?" *Harvard Business Review,* 1982, 60, 105–114.

Naylor, T. H., and Tapon, F. "The Capital Asset Pricing Model: An Evaluation of its Potential as a Strategic Management Tool." *Management Science,* 1982, 28 (10), 1166–1173.

Palepu, K. "Diversification Strategy, Profit Performance, and the Entropy Measure." *Strategic Management Journal,* 1985, 6, 239–255.

Pitts, R. A., and Hopkins, H. D. "Firm Diversity: Conceptualization and Measurement." *Academy of Management Review*, 1984, 7, 620–629.

Rumelt, R. P. *Strategy, Structure, and Economic Performance*. Cambridge, Mass.: Harvard University, Division of Research, 1974.

Salter, M. S., and Weinhold, W. A. "Diversification via Acquisition: Creating Value."*Harvard Business Review*, July-August 1978, 166–176.

Sharpe, W. F. "Capital Asset Prices: A Theory of Market Equilibrium Under Conditions of Risk." *Journal of Finance*, 1964, 425–442.

Slovic, P., Fischhoff, B., and Lichtenstein, S. "Behavioral Decision Theory." *Annual Review of Psychology*, 1977, 28, 425–442.

Stahl, M. J., and Zimmerer, T. W. "Modeling Strategic Acquisition Policies: A Simulation of Executives' Acquisition Decisions." *Academy of Management Journal*, 1984, 27, 369–386.

Thompson, A. A., and Strickland, A. J. *Strategy and Policy: Concepts and Cases*. Plano, Tex.: Business Publications, 1981.

Tobin, J. "Liquidity Preference as Behavior Towards Risk." *Review of Economic Studies*, 1958, 25, 65–85.

Venkatraman, N., and Camillus, J. "Exploring the Concept of Fit in Strategic Management." *Academy of Management Review*, 1984, 9, 513–525.

CHAPTER 6

Long-term Performance of Conglomerate and Related Diversification

Many business policy texts discuss strategic fit as a key concept in formulating business strategy (Venkatraman and Camillus, 1984). The concept is concerned with the similarity of a new business venture to the firm's existing line(s) of business. Indeed, Thompson and Strickland (1981) present a detailed discussion of strategic fit in terms of operating fit, product/market fit, and management fit. They question whether a firm should be involved in a business venture if it cannot be placed in one of the three preceding categories. They argue that synergy usually results if strategic fit occurs. This becomes the theoretical justification for related diversification. Indeed, "sticking to their knitting and doing what they know best" is a characteristic of excellent firms (Peters and Waterman, 1982).

On the other hand, adherents of the Capital Asset Pricing Model (CAPM) argue that the CAPM should be used as a strategy formulation tool (Naylor and Tapon, 1982). Chapters 3, 4 and 5 test the CAPM with data from three different samples involving several hundred executives with three different instruments. Those studies indicate that executives do *not* use the CAPM as a strategy formulation tool. The CAPM theorizes that a firm should combine divisions or strategic business units that are not related to each other, or are negatively related to each other, in order to reduce financial risk (Mullins, 1982). Indeed, Marshall, Yauritz and Greenberg (1984) specifically argued that the CAPM is the theoretical justification for conglomerate diversification.

Bettis (1983) has recently pointed out the paradox between the CAPM and strategic fit. He concluded that research should address the paradox.

This chapter was written by Michael J. Stahl and Alok Srivastava of Georgia State University. An earlier version was presented at the Southern Management Association meeting in November 1985, in Orlando, Fla., and published in the *Proceedings*, pp. 70–72.

This chapter empirically tests the opposing concepts of the CAPM and strategic fit by examining the long-term performance of conglomerate and related diversification.

Here is the contradiction between strategic fit and the CAPM. Strategic fit argues that r_{jm} (equation 3.2) should be positive; hence, the firm is relatedly diversified. The CAPM argues that r_{jm} should be zero or negative; hence, the firm is a conglomerate. The purpose of this chapter is to see which concept of r_{jm} yields better corporate performance in the long term. The null hypothesis is that the relatedly diversified firms perform better than the conglomerates.

METHODOLOGY

Several studies (Bettis and Hall, 1982; Curley, 1971; Evans and Archer, 1968; Haugen and Langetieg, 1975; Lev and Mandelker, 1970; Mason and Goudzward, 1976; Melicher and Rush, 1973; Reinhardt, 1972) have examined the performance of these two forms of diversification. However, many of the studies are deficient because they use too short a time period, or inadequately classify the firms into the two categories, or simulate performance, or measure performance too narrowly (Pitts and Hopkins, 1982).

A commonly used measure to examine long-term corporate performance is growth in earnings per share (EPS) (Curley, 1971; Reinhardt, 1972). But this "bottom line" measure is not the only relevant measure of corporate long-term performance especially in the case of conglomerates (Lev and Mandelker, 1970; Levy and Sarnat, 1971; Salter and Weinhold, 1978). It is argued that conglomerates diversify business risk. A measure for comparison of overall business risk is the stock's beta. Since the overall business risk is highly influenced by the financial risk due to use of leverage, no comparison of risk is complete if a measure of financial risk, like the debt to equity (D/E) ratio is not compared (Lev and Mandelker, 1970). Salter and Weinhold (1978) argue that the price earnings ratio (P/E) is of great interest in diversifications because of the uncertainty of whether the market will value the conglomerate at the P/E of the acquiring firm, or of the acquired firm, or some average. Common measures of long-term corporate performance reported in *Business Week's* Annual Corporate Scoreboard, *Forbes,* and *Fortune's* 500 listing are profitability (return on equity and return on capital) and growth in sales. All performance measures were obtained from the *Forbes* "36th Annual Report on American Industry" (1984).

Overall, this research examines seven measures in the three areas of profitability, growth and risk. Profitability was examined in two ways—return on equity (ROE) and return on capital (ROC). Each was the five-year (1979-1983) average percentage. Growth was examined in two ways—growth in sales and growth in earnings per share (EPS). Each was the five-year (1979-1983) compounded annual rate of growth. Two separate measures of financial interest were captured—debt to equity (D/E) and price earnings ratio (P/E). Both were for 1983. D/E was reported at the end of the fiscal year. P/E was the average for the latest fiscal year. D/E was examined to reflect the financial risk of the firms. P/E was used to reflect the market's perception of the firm's potential earnings. Finally, the stocks' beta values were compared to study the level of business risk of the two groups.

The Fortune 500 Sample

All firms studied were Fortune 500 firms in 1984. In its "Annual Report on American Industry," *Forbes* classified firms employing a growth strategy of conglomerate diversification into two categories: multi-companies and conglomerates. The only distinction between these categories is that the multi-companies had been inactive in the acquisition front in the year for which the report was published. All firms from the combined list of multi-companies and conglomerates published in *Forbes'* report that were also in the Fortune 500 list of 1984 formed the sample of 42 conglomerates.

Forbes does not classify firms by those employing a strategy of related diversification. The criteria used in this research to classify related diversification were several. First, the firm should have business operations in at least two distinct industry segments. Second, not more than 95 percent of sales should be derived from any one line of business (Rumelt, 1974). Third, all lines of business should be related from the product point of view (Pitts and Hopkins, 1982; Thompson and Strickland, 1981). This determination was made from the firm's description of business lines in *Moody's Industrial Manual* (1984). Fourth, the firm should be a Fortune 500 firm. These criteria yielded a list of 175 relatedly diversified firms. Vertically integrated firms are essentially single industry businesses and do not meet the prerequisites of related diversification, that is, concentric and horizontal diversification.

RESULTS

Table 6.1 contains the averages between the relatedly diversified firms and the conglomerates for the seven performance measures. Since several measures were compared, a multivariate analysis of variance (MANOVA) was performed first. An F ratio of 3.09 (p < .01) indicated that there were significant overall differences between the two corporate strategies. Specifically, the relatedly diversified firms performed better. As Table 6.1 indicates, seven separate t-tests were then performed. The 175 relatedly diversified firms had a higher ROC, a higher growth in sales, and a significantly lower D/E ratio than the 42 conglomerates.

Table 6.1
Average Performance Measures for Related and Conglomerate Diversification

Performance Measure	Related Diversification[a]	Conglomerate Diversification[b]	t
ROE	14.85	13.97	0.74
ROC	11.83	10.40	1.60*
Sales Growth	13.17	10.09	2.14*
EPS Growth	6.78	6.80	0.05
D/E	0.37	0.54	3.12**
PE	16.57	14.68	1.42
Stock Beta	1.02	1.06	0.78

[a] $n_1 = 175$.

[b] $n_2 = 42$.

*$p < .05$.

**$p < .01$.

CONCLUSIONS

This research was undertaken to test for differences in long-term corporate performance between relatedly diversified and conglomerate firms. Tests of 42 conglomerates versus 175 relatedly diversified firms, all from the Fortune 500 list, demonstrated that related diversification is a more effective long-term strategy. The relatedly diversified strategies were associated with higher profitability, higher growth in sales and less financial risk due to lower financial leverage. This finding of less risk and higher profitability is fascinating because adherents of the CAPM argue that one is usually traded off for the other. These data refute the dictates of the CAPM and support the concept of strategic fit.

Contrary to the CAPM, the two samples did not differ significantly when business risk, as reflected in the firm's stock beta values, was examined. Also contrary to the CAPM, the financial risk (D/E) of the conglomerates was higher than that of the relatedly diversified firms. Varadarajan and Ramanujam (1987) recently examined the effect of related and unrelated diversification on profitability and growth measure. They used an innovative method to classify firms as related or unrelated based on two-digit and four-digit Standard Industrial Classification (SIC) codes. They reported that the relatedly diversified firms were more effective than the unrelatedly diversified. However, they neglected to examine the effect of diversification on risk.

Since the conglomerates operate with a much lower equity base, their profitability did not differ from that of the relatedly diversified firms when the profitability measure was ROE. However, the relatedly diversified firms were significantly more profitable when the profitability measure was ROC. The relatedly diversified companies made more profitable use of the total capital employed. Future studies should take this into account when comparing profitability of different diversification strategies.

Perhaps Mueller (1969) is correct that the primary reason for conglomerate merger is to maximize the income of top management which is typically tied to sales or asset growth. The data in this chapter argue that profitability (ROC), sales growth, and financial risk (D/E) are superior in relatedly diversified firms. These data provide further rationale that firms should "stick to their knitting" as Peters and Waterman (1982) argued in their popular book, *In Search of Excellence*. Many businesses seem to have realized this. Recent *Business Week* articles on February 6, 1984, and March 21, 1988, stated that there are more relatedly based mergers today than the mistaken conglomerate mergers of the past.

REFERENCES

Bettis, R. A. "Modern Financial Theory, Corporate Strategy and Public Policy: Three Conundrums." *Academy of Management Review,* 1983, 8 (3), 406-415.

Bettis, R. A., and Hall, W. K. "Diversification Strategy, Accounting Determined Risk, and Accounting Determined Return." *Academy of Management Journal,* 1982, 25 (2), 254-264.

Business Week. "How the New Merger Will Benefit the Economy." 6 February 1984, pp. 42-54.

Curley, Anthony J. "Conglomerate Earnings Per Share: Real and Transitory Growth." *The Accounting Review,* 1971, 46 (3), 519-528.

Dobrzynski, J. "Learning from the Mangled Mergers of the Past." *Business Week,* 21 March 1988, p. 126.

Evans, J. L., and Archer, S. H. "Diversification and the Reduction of Dispersion: An Empirical Analysis." *Journal of Finance,* 1968, 23, 761-767.

Haugen, R. A., and Langetieg, T.C. "An Empirical Test for Synergism in Mergers." *Journal of Finance,* September 1975, 1003-1014.

Lev, B., and Mandelker, G. "The Microeconomic Consequences of Corporate Mergers." *Journal of Finance,* 1970. 25 (4), 791-802.

Levy, H., and Sarnat, M. "Diversification, Portfolio Analysis, and the Uneasy Case of Conglomerate Mergers." *Journal of Finance*, 1971, 26 (2), 521-537.

Marshall, W. J., Yauritz, J. B., and Greenberg, E. "Incentives for Diversification and the Structure of the Conglomerate Firm." *Southern Economic Journal,* 1984, 51 (1), 1-23.

Mason, H. R., and Goudzward, M. "Performance of Conglomerate Firms: A Portfolio Approach." *Journal of Finance,* 1976, 31, 39-48.

Melicher, R. W., and Rush, D. F. "The Performance of Conglomerate Firms: Recent Risk and Return Experience." *Journal of Finance,* May 1973, 381-388.

Mueller, D. C. "A Theory of Conglomerate Mergers." *Quarterly Journal of Economics,* November 1969, 643-660.

Mullins, D. W. "Does the Capital Asset Pricing Model Work?" *Harvard Business Review,* 1982, 60, 105-114.

Naylor, T. H., and Tapon, R.. "The Capital Asset Pricing Model: An Evaluation of Its Potential as a Strategic Planning Tool." *Management Science,* 1982, 28, 1166-1173.

Peters, J. T., and Waterman, R. N. *In Search of Excellence.* New York: Harper and Row, 1982.

Pitts, R. A., and Hopkins, H. D. "Firm Diversity: Conceptualization and Measurement." *Academy of Management Review,* 1982, 4, 620-629.

Reinhardt, U. E. "Conglomerate EPS: Immediate and Post Merger Effects." *The Accounting Review,* 1972, 47 (2), 360-370.

Rumelt, R. P. *Strategy, Structure and Economic Performance.* Boston: Harvard Business School, Division of Research, 1974.

Salter, M. S., and Weinhold, W. A. "Diversification Via Acquisitions: Creating Value." *Harvard Business Review,* July-August 1978, 166

Standard & Poor's Register of Corporations, Directors and Executives (Vol. 1). New York: Standard and Poor's Corp., 1984.

Thompson, A. A., Jr., and Strickland, A. H. *Strategy and Policy: Concepts and Cases.* Rev. ed. Plano, Tex. Business Publications, Inc., 1981.

Varadarajan, P. R., and Ramanujam, V. "Diversification and Performance: A Reexamination Using a New Two-Dimensional Conceptualization of Diversity in Firms." *Academy of Management Journal,* 1987, 30 (2), 380-393.

Venkatraman, N., and Camillus, J. "Exploring the Concept of Fit in Strategic Management." *Academy of Management Review,* 1984, 9, 513-525.

CHAPTER 7

Joint Venture Decisions

JOINT VENTURE STRATEGIES

In the realm of corporate-level strategies, joint ventures recently have gained much attention in corporations as a viable ownership alternative. Indeed, a recent issue of *Business Week* (1986) featured joint ventures as a strategy on the cover. This was not always true. Less than a decade ago, joint venture was viewed as a last (external) organizational form prior to merger (Berg and Friedman, 1978). Today, however, a renewed and sustained level of new joint venture activity exists. Peak joint venture activity occurred in 1972 with a total of 275 new joint ventures reported by the Federal Trade Commission. This number fell to 269 new joint ventures in 1983. New joint ventures reported to the FTC have since been maintained around the 1983 level.

Findings and experience in the literature on both domestic and international joint ventures have tended to focus on motives for joint venture (Berg and Friedman, 1978; Brodley, 1982; Cozzolino, 1981; Katz, 1984; Pfeffer and Norwak, 1976; Roberts, 1980; Roulac, 1980); financial considerations (Berg and Friedman, 1981; Duncan, 1982; Hewitt, 1979); implementation issues (Harrigan, 1985; Peterson and Shimada, 1978); structural issues (Berg and Friedman, 1980, 1981; Harrigan, 1985); and environmental issues (Peterson and Shimada, 1978; Reynolds, 1978; Sullivan and Peterson, 1982). Much of the literature on joint venture has been conceptual in nature and has served as a theoretical construct upon which to do empirical research.

This chapter was written by Rebecca I. Porterfield of Mississippi State University and Michael J. Stahl. An earlier version was presented at the 1986 National Academy of Management meeting in Chicago.

Two comprehensive empirical studies of joint ventures were conducted by Berg and Friedman (1978, 1980, 1981) and Harrigan (1985). Harrigan relied on a normative approach of telephone and field interviews. Berg and Friedman likewise utilized interviews coupled with surveys and questionnaires. A major contribution of these research endeavors has been to better delineate the strategic decision criteria corporate planners utilize in weighing the benefits and costs of joint ventures as cooperating strategies.

Roulac (1980) conceptually identified four strategic decision criteria for entering into a joint venture: The minimizing of risk and maximizing of available diverse resources, the integration of separate business firms to provide for socially desirable efficiencies, new technology and entrepreneurial commitment, and the circumvention of capital crisis.

In their survey-questionnaire data, Berg and Friedman (1978) found that acquisition know-how, research and development, feedstock supplies, and exploration of patents all ranked high in reasons for co-venturing with another firm. Additionally, market penetration ranked high in engineering firms and performance of product output ranked low in engineering and chemical firms. Financial considerations also ranked low in engineering and chemical firms. Berg and Friedman and Harrigan found that backward integration was given as the major reason for joint venture in the chemical industry.

Harrigan's more recent investigation of the motives for entering a joint venture is compatible with Berg and Friedman, and Roulac. Harrigan delineated Berg and Friedman's and Roulac's motives into fewer subsets, but the broad concepts are similar. Harrigan segmented motives for joint ventures into internal uses, competitive uses, and strategic uses. Internal uses tie closely to financial return, financial risk minimization, and knowledge acquisition through entrepreneurial employees. Competitive uses include multiple identifications of market penetration practices, as well as efficiencies through backward integration. Strategic uses encompass technology acquisition and vertical integration.

A major problem with the prior joint venture empirical studies is the use of questionable methodologies. The literature on decision making consistently indicates that humans do not have accurate insight into how they make multiple criteria decisions (Newell and Simon, 1972; Slovic and Lichtenstein, 1971; Slovic, Fischhoff, and Lichtenstein, 1977; Stahl and Zimmerer, 1984). Thus, the methodologies using interviews and surveys (Berg and Friedman, 1977, 1978, 1981) may be asking more than the subjects can accurately report. Second, the literature also indicates that direct questioning of subjects may be prone to a social desirability response bias in which the subject provides an "acceptable" or "appropriate" answer, whereas, decision modeling is not prone to such a bias (Arnold and Feldman, 1981; Stahl and Harrell, 1982). If the methodologies used in prior joint venture studies are suspect, how much credence can be put in their results? Therefore, the purpose of this research is to develop and test a joint venture decision model using decision modeling as a research methodology.

Two research areas were investigated to gain insight into this corporate strategy. The first was to ascertain if there was identifiable consistency among groups of strategic planners in determining joint venture co-partners. This provided insight into decision criteria they relate to differing groups. The second area of investigation related various decision criteria to financial indicators. These tests provided understanding of the relationships between decision criteria of strategic decision makers and the firm's outcome in terms of financial effectiveness. To evaluate these areas under investigation, the following five hypotheses were tested:

H1: Joint venture decision criteria are consistent across industrial groups.

H2: Joint venture decision criteria are consistent among strategic planners with similar functional experience bases.

H3: Joint venture decision criteria are consistent among strategic planners who perceive their corporate scope is the same.

H4: Strategic planners' actual joint venture criteria weights are consistent with their perceived (subjective) criteria weights (equations 1.2 and 1.3).

H5: There are no significant relationships between joint venture criteria and performance measures either at the joint venture partner (parent) level or at the firm (child) level.

METHODOLOGY

The Joint Venture Exercise

Policy capturing the decision to enter into a joint venture at the time actual criteria are evaluated would be an ideal way to determine which criteria are used and what weights they represent in the decision process. However, as this is not possible, we simulated the decision criteria.

This decision exercise developed presents various potential joint venture partner scenarios in terms of five decision criteria. The five decision cues were derived from the works of Berg and Friedman (1978, 1981), Roulac (1980), and Harrigan (1985). The five decision cues are technology/knowledge acquisition (TK), market penetration (MP), supplier protection/backward integration (BI), financial return (FRT), and financial risk minimization (FRI).

The exercise was designed as an orthogonal experiment with two cue levels set high ($+1$) or low (-1) to preserve orthogonality. Based on the cue levels, the subject was requested to evaluate his/her preference for entering into the simulated joint venture by circling a value along a scale of -5 to $+5$. A sample candidate firm is given in Figure 7.1.

Thirty-two different simulated joint venture scenarios were presented. This represents five decision cues, each at two levels (high and low), or a $2 \times 2 \times 2 \times 2 \times 2$ full factorial experiment.

Additionally, each planner was asked to evaluate his/her subjective weight on each of the criteria apart from the 32 decisions. These were

Figure 7.1
Sample Candidate Firm

<u>Joint Venture Candidate Number 12</u>

<u>Technology/Knowledge</u> — The degree to which the candidate
firm provides technology or knowledge acquisition through
direct patent or indirect expert staff support is   LOW

<u>Market Penetration</u> — The degree to which market penetration
will be enhanced via the joint venture candidate is   HIGH

<u>Supplier Protection/Backward Integration</u> — The degree to
which the joint venture firm will protect supply flow and
cost economies is   LOW

<u>Financial Assistance</u> — The degree to which the joint
venture will induce a greater return on investment than
your firm's individual effort is   LOW

<u>Risk Minimization</u> — The degree to which financial risk is
spread due to shared or pooled interest is   LOW

Indicate your preference for entering into a joint venture
with the described firm by circling the number which
indicates your opinion below:

  -5   -4   -3   -2   -1   -0   +1   +2   +3   +4   +5

Strongly Recommend   Strongly Recommend
Against Approval   Approval of
Of Joint Venture   Joint Venture

---

obtained by instructing the participant to spread a total of 100 points
among the five decision criteria based on relative importance. These scores
provided insight into the subjective decision making of the subjects.

At the end of the decision exercise, background information needed for
hypothesis testing was requested of the subjects. Financial data needed were
requested via a multiple choice format over ranged financial effectiveness
indicators. This was done to increase the response of confidential information and to minimize the completion time of the test instrument as an incen-
tive to answer all questions. Industrial classifications requested were based
on the classification system used in the 1984 *Business Week Scoreboard*. All
respondents who so requested were provided individual feedback on their
decision exercises to increase response rate.

The Sampled Corporate Planners

A random sample of 1,500 members of the North American Society for Corporate Planners (NASCP) was drawn. (This sample was different from those used in Chapters 3, 4 and 5.) The 1,500 was reduced to 1,306 by dropping corporate libraries and non-corporate entities. According to NASCP, the total membership of this organization is about 6,000 of which 19 percent are vice-presidents, 24 percent are directors, and 26 perecnt are managers. This society was utilized as its professional members are actively involved in decision policy formulation for their organizations. NASCP reported that 60 percent of its members have designed and administered strategic planning processes, 57 percent have reviewed and evaluated strategies, and 41 percent supported acquisitions and divestitures. In addition, 72 percent of the membership represent corporations with over $51 million in sales annually. This group was thus identified as instrumental in any joint venture decision.

Of the 1,306 decision exercises that were sent out, 253 responses were received representing a 19.4 percent response rate. Of the 253, 187 were completed and useful responses. Of the respondents, 85.6 percent reported sales volumes greater than $60 million annually, comparing favorably with population statistics. Sixty-five percent of the respondents had over five years experience in strategic planning, with 54 percent of them personally involved in joint venture decisions. Eighty percent of the firms represented by the respondents had participated in joint ventures with 39 percent reporting domestic and international joint venture activity levels of over five. Marketing and finance represented the primary functional areas in which the respondents spent most of their careers (17 percent each). Thirteen industries were reported with five or more firms and 66 percent of the firms represented indicated their firms were international in scope. The demographic linkages between the sample and the population indicated that the sample was representative.

RESULTS
Analysis

Individual regression models were run for each of the 187 respondents with all two-level interaction effects. Also, a group model regression analysis was performed by grouping all 187 respondents into one regression.

All main effects and three of the two-way interaction effects were statistically significant at the .01 significance level in the group model. The same three interactions were found statistically significant at the .01 level in 30 percent of the individual regression models for the market penetration-technology/knowledge acquisition interaction, 11 percent for the market penetration-financial risk minimization interaction, and 13 percent for the technology/knowledge acquisition-financial risk minimization interaction.

For this reason, all subsequent analyses for hypothesis testing were completed twice. Models with the five main effects only and models with the five main effects and the three significant interaction effects were tested independently. Although three interactions were significant, the net effect of these two sets of analysis was that the three significant interaction effects explained only about 5 percent of the total variance of the models under investigation. Little additional insight into the decision criteria was gained. Therefore, only the main effects are reported in this chapter.

The next step was to check for the internal consistency of the decision makers (Stahl and Harrell, 1982). The average R^2 for all 187 subjects was .83 for the main effects model. In order to ensure an internal consistency level significant at the .05 level, individual R^2s needed to be at least .46 for the individual regression models. Three individual main effects models exhibited R^2s below .46 and were dropped from further analysis due to their level of inconsistency.

Industrial Decision Criteria

As the decision makers exhibited high internal consistency, they were then aggregrated by industrial group and regression models were run on all industry groups. Only those industrial groups with five or more firms were analyzed for cross-industry comparison. To test for differences in decision criteria, a Chow's F test on the regression models was completed for all industries taken two at a time. For example, the chemicals (N = 13) and conglomerates (N = 15) were fitted to one model with 896 observations and a Chow's F test was calculated. All possible two-way industrial combinations were checked for and all proved different from each other at the .01 level. Thus, the null hypothesis was rejected that decision criteria are consistent across industrial groups. The average relative weights by industry by decision criteria are found in Table 7.1.

Evaluating industrial decision criteria by the magnitude of the relative weights provides immediate preliminary information. These findings indicate the chemical industry puts very little value in joint venture partners who could potentially provide backward integration. In fact, all industries placed little relative weight on backward integration in their decision models. Alternately, nearly all placed high value on market penetration, technology/knowledge acquisition, and financial risk. Surprisingly, financial return was valued low in all decision models with the exception of metals and mining.

Functional Experiential Similarities/Disparities

Hypothesis 2 was structured to test for decision criteria preference on work experience derived from a functional orientation. Eight functional areas were provided in the background information. A ninth category,

Table 7.1.
Average Relative Weights by Industry

Industries	Market Penetration	Technology/ Knowledge Acquisition	Background Integration	Financial Risk Min.	Financial Return
Banks and Holding Cos. (N=5)	15	32	2	43	8
Chemicals (N=13)	19	44	5	22	10
Conglomerates (N=15)	26	35	5	28	6
Electrical and Electronics (N=12)	32	40	5	15	8
Utilities (N=10)	22	15	8	41	14
Metals and Mining (N=5)	23	22	7	26	22
Nonbank Financial (N=6)	11	43	4	41	1
Other (N=36)	27	36	8	21	8
Office Equipment and Computers (N≠7)	46	21	6	22	5
Oil Service and Supply (N=5)	32	33	3	18	14
Paper and Forest Products (N=5)	38	24	2	31	5
Service Industries (N=14)	26	37	6	19	12
Miscellaneous Manufacturing (N=5)	21	46	2	26	5
Average Weights by all industries	26	34	6	26	8
Standard deviation	22	23	7	24	13

Note: Only industries with five or more sampled firms are reported.

Multiple Functions was added for analytic purposes because 27 respondents checked more than one background. The 187 subjects were aggregated by functional groups and regression models were run for each group. Chow's F tests on functional models taken two at a time were calculated. All models were found statistically different at the .01 level except finance and other models. To further identify these group differences, the average relative weights for each functional group were calculated. These calculated values are found in Table 7.2.

Table 7.2
Average Relative Weights by Function

Function	Market Penetration	Technology/ Knowledge Acquisition	Backward Integration	Financial Risk Minimization	Financial Return
Marketing (N=31)	30	38	4	23	5
Sales (N=1)	29	33	11	23	4
Administra- tion (N=19)	21	37	5	28	9
Accounting (N=8)	25	23	4	24	24
Finance (N=32)	25	35	6	26	8
Other (N=49)	26	35	5	26	8
Research and Development (N=6)	18	17	10	44	11
Manufacturing/ Operations (N=36)	29	30	8	24	9
Multiple (N=27)	26	39	6	23	6

As in the industrial classifications, examination of the relationship of the relative weights yields preliminary insight into the decision process. Overall, the three decision cues, market penetration (MP), technology/knowledge acquisition (TK), and financial risk minimization (FRI) exhibited the greater relative weight values. The TK cue was highest in all but two of the functions—accounting and research development. Research and development placed very high emphasis on financial risk. With the exception of the accounting background subjects, financial return was universally low. These findings have intuitive appeal. Given accountants' trained orientations, it would seem reasonable that they would place more emphasis on a co-venture partner who could provide a good financial return. Likewise, the low relative weight placed on the TK cue and high value placed on FRI by the research and development subjects seems logical. Research and development subjects might well feel that TK would be their offering to a co-venturer in exchange for financial risk reduction.

Table 7.3
Average Relative Weights by Scope

Scope	Market Penetration	Technology/ Knowledge Acquisition	Backward Integration	Financial Risk Minimization	Financial Return
Regional (N=27)	18	32	6	31	13
National (N=35)	25	29	6	31	9
International (N=122)	28	36	6	23	7

Decision Criteria Based on Corporate Scope

Corporate scope in this research refers to the perception of the strategic planner as to whether the respondent believes his or her firm to be regional, national, or international in its outlook; 28 subjects responded as regional, 35 as national, and 123 responded as international.

Regression models were formulated for the three groups of respondents sorted by scope. The Chow's F test indicated all three groups were statistically different at the .01 significance level. Relative weights were calculated and are found in Table 7.3. Like the industrial groups, backward integration and financial return are lower than market penetration, technology/knowledge acquisition, and financial risk minimization. This finding is compatible with the notion of global industries seeking market penetration or expansion (Harrigan, 1985).

Relative Weight vs. Subjective Weight Criteria

Upon completion of the decision exercise, all respondents were requested to spread 100 points over the five cues found in the decision exercise. The scores placed on each of these five factors are the respondents' subjective weights—the values they feel they placed on each of the cues. Comparison of subjective versus relative weights provides insight into the decision maker's ability to understand his/her decision process.

Five paired t-tests were completed for all respondents on relative weights versus subjective weights. Four of the relative weights were significantly different than the associated subjective weights indicating poor insight by the decision makers into their own decision making process. This is consistent with prior research findings (Slovic, Fischhoff, and Lichtenstein, 1977; Chapters 2, 10, 11, 12).

Table 7.4
Comparison of Average Relative and Subjective Weights

Cue	Relative Weight	Subjective Weight	t
Market Penetration	25.8	26.9	-0.49
Technology/Knowledge Acquisition	34.4	25.6	4.08*
Backward Integration	5.7	10.6	-10.45*
Financial Risk Minimization	25.9	13.3	7.22*
Financial Return	8.2	23.86	-12.35*

*p < 01.

Note: n = 184.

Financial Data Ties

All respondents were asked to provide parent company return on sales, return on investment, joint venture child return on sales, and certain financial relationships between parent and child. The data were sorted first by participants and non-participants in joint venture activity and then by industy, joint venture maturity, and other sorts as needed. Two sample t-tests showed no statistical differences between the groups with one key exception: 76 of the 106 firms with joint venture experience reported their joint venture child experienced lower ROIs than did the parent firm. Additionally, the average return on sales for the joint venture child ranged from 0-8.99 percent. This appears rather low and is compatible with the low relative weight placed on the financial return cue found in the decision exercise.

To determine if any relationship existed between the decision criteria and the financial effectiveness measures, a correlation analysis was performed. The correlation analysis indicated very few significant relationships. The strongest relationship, that of a negative correlation between ROI (parent) and the financial return cue, suggests that as the decision makers put less and less weight on financial return, their ROI moves up. A positive relationship between the profit to sales of the parent and market penetration was also observed.

CONCLUSIONS AND DISCUSSION

The findings in this study indicate that joint ventures are not only alive and well, but are healthy, viable strategic alternatives. With 80 percent of all

Table 7.5
Correlations of Decision Criteria and Performance
Measures for Both Joint Venture Parent and Child

	Market Penetration	Technology/ Knowledge Acquisition	Backward Integration	Financial Risk Minimization	Financial Return
Profit to Sales (Child)	-0.02	0.10	-0.03	-0.04	-0.03
Profit to Sales (Parent)	0.16*	-0.06	-0.05	-0.10	-0.07
ROI (Parent)	0.07	0.03	-0.09	-0.02	-0.22**
Change in Sales (Parent)	0.08	0.03	0.02	-0.04	-0.14

*p < 0.05.
**p < 0.01.

Note: n = 184.

respondents involved in joint venture activity and 39 percent of these reporting activity levels of over five joint ventures, the degree to which this co-venture strategy is utilized becomes readily apparent. Respondents who had personally been involved in a joint venture were asked if they would consider entering a new joint venture and 103 responded yes while only 3 responded no. Contrary to the negative motivations for joint venture and the high rate of failure (40–50 percent), the strategic planners reported very pro–joint venture attitudes.

The primary purpose of this research was to determine those characteristics most sought by strategic planners in selecting co-venture partners. Berg and Friedman (1978) and Harrigan (1985) suggested that certain industries seek partners for strategic purposes. Specifically, the chemical and steel industries seek backward integration as an protectionist measure of supplier/cost and scalar economies. Harrigan (1985) also discussed the concept of global industries seeking markets through joint venture activities. The findings in this study shed new light on the industrial decision patterns investigated by Berg and Friedman and Harrigan. Industrial groupings indicated three primary attributes desired in joint venture partners: market penetration, technology/knowledge acquistion, and the spreading of financial risk. The chemical industry was not alone in weighting backward integration as very low in decision criteria importance. All industries averaged together gave backward integration one-third the weight of each of the primary attributes above. There may be many reasons for this dichotomy. The most important reason may be the methodology itself. The research of Berg and Friedman and Harrigan utilized surveys, questionnaires, and interviews as a basis for their findings. These methodologies only allow the researcher insight into the decision process after it has transpired. As in many situations, when the human mind is asked to re-capture the thought process utilized in making prior decisions, that recall may be marred by subsequent events and thoughts that distort the original process. This concept is known as the social desirability response bias. Arnold and Feldman (1981) found social desirability bias to affect self-report where choices or decisions are required. The methodology used in this study has been shown to eliminate social desirability response bias (Stahl and Harrell, 1982). The differences between the relative and subjective weights repeated for four of the five cues underline possible distortions in direct questioning methodologies (subjective weights).

The scope of the firms in this study exhibits differences in preferred attributes for co-venture choices. It seems reasonable that international firms would seek market penetration as a primary attribute in seeking a co-venture partner. The works of Jordan (1983) and Harrigan (1985) support this thesis. Evidence from this research serves to corroborate further this finding as relative weights for market penetration were statistically higher for internationals than for regionals.

The functional experience analysis clearly indicates that decision makers in certain functions bring to the decision process a distinct orientation based upon the experience base from which they have primarily operated. Planners of multiple functions experience show no marked contrasts in their decision process over all planners in general. Accountants, as a group, put as much weight on the financial return cue as they did on market penetration, technology/knowledge acquisition, and financial risk minimization. Research and development placed significantly lower weight on technology/knowledge acquisition than all other functions. Perhaps it was this "global" perspective based on diverse experience that allowed for a more universal approach by the multiple experience group. When strategy decisions such as joint venture are formulated, the outcome of this research suggests a need for a broader experience base to reduce bias that might be myopic in nature.

The financial information gleaned from this study was mixed. The reported financial measures for the parent firm and the joint venture child indicated a lower return on sales by the joint venture child and lower ROIs for the child. A postive relationship between the profit to sales of the parent and market penetration was observed. Apparently, attention to market penetration may lead to sales profitability.

Overall, this research indicates that market penetration, technology/knowledge acquisition, and financial risk minimization are important to the joint venture decision as these three cues were weighted on average three to five times higher than financial return and backward integration. Research in this area should continue to test these three variables against newly considered criteria as the evolutionary process of business activity continues. Future longitudinal studies of the financial effectiveness measures of these firms against the measured decision criteria of this study would add further insight into the decision process.

Postscript on Joint Ventures

During a three-week lecture tour of the People's Republic of China in late 1987, the book's author had interviews, and discussions with many Chinese managers and educators in Beijing, Shanghai and Wuxi. The findings of this chapter concerning the important decision criteria for joint ventures were supported there.

To say that technology acquisition is important to the Chinese would be a dramatic understatement. They know that in many industries they are technologically behind other world competitors. The Cultural Revolution of 1966-1976 did not exactly help them to catch up. Many Chinese understand the technology acquisition benefits of joint ventures and are not bashful about entering into such temporary business arrangements for the sake of acquiring the technology. If the Chinese managers and educators who were met on that trip had completed this joint venture exercise, they most likely would have placed nearly a 100 percent relative weight on technology acquisition as a reason for entering a joint venture to the exclusion of the other criteria. As business is becoming more international in scope, more needs to be known about the decision criteria used by our international joint venture partners.

REFERENCES

Arnold, H. J., and Feldman, D. C. "Social Desirability Bias in Self-Report Choice Situations." *Academy of Management Journal,* 1981, 24, 377-385.

Berg, S., and Friedman, P. "Joint Venture Competition, and Technological Complementaries from Chemicals." *Southern Economic Journal,* 1977, 43, 133-137.

Berg, S., and Friedman, P. "Joint Ventures in American Industry." *Mergers and Acquisitions,* 1978, 13(2), 28-41.

Berg, S., and Friedman, P. "Joint Venture in American Industry Part III-Public Policy Issues." *Mergers and Acquisitions,* 1979, 13(4), 18-29.

Berg, S., and Friedman, P. "Corporate Courtship and Successful Joint Ventures." *California Management Review,* 1980, 22, 85-91.

Berg, S., and Friedman, P. "Impacts of Domestic Venture on Industry." *Review of Economic Statistics,* 1981, 63, 293-298.

Brodley, J. "Joint Ventures and Antitrust Policy." *Harvard Law Review,* 1982, 95(7), 1521-1590.

Cozzolino, J. "Joint Venture Risk—How to Determine Your Share." *Mergers and Acquisitions,* 1981, 16(3), 35-39.

Duncan, J. "Impacts of New Entry and Horizontal Joint Ventures on Industrial Rates of Return." *The Review of Economics and Statistics,* 1982, 64, 339-343.

Harrell, A. M., and Stahl, M. J. "A Behavioral Decision Theory Approach for Measuring McClelland's Trichotomy of Needs." *Journal of Applied Psychology,* 1981, 66, 242-247.

Harrigan, K. R. *Strategies for Joint Ventures.* Lexington, Mass.: Lexington Books, 1985.

Hewitt, H. "Loss Allocation Denied Effect When Not the Same as Profits." *Journal of Taxation,* 1979, 21(2), 118.

Jordan, R. "Targeting International Marketing." *Telecommunications,* 1983, 17(4), 88-92.

Katz, M. "The American Small Car is Fading." *Business Week,* March 19, 1984, 88-96.

Levine, J., and Byrne, J. "Corporate Odd Couples." *Business Week.* 21 July, 1986, pp. 100-105.

Newell, A., and Simon, H. A. *Human Problem Solving.* Englewood Cliffs, New Jersey: Prentice-Hall, 1972.

Peterson, R., and Shimada, J. "Sources of Management Problems in Japanese-American Joint Venture." *Academy of Management,* 1978, 3, 796-804.

Pfeffer, J., and Norwak, P. "Patterns of Venture Activity—Implications for Antitrust Policy." *Antitrust Bulletin,* 1976, 21(2), 315-339.

Reynolds, J. "Developing Policy Responses to Cultural Differences." *Business Horizons,* 1978, 21(4), 28-35.

Roberts, E. "New Ventures for Corporate Growth." *Harvard Business Review,* July-August 1980, 134-142.

Roulac, S. "Structuring the Joint Venture." *Mergers and Acquisitions,* 1980, 15(1), 4-14.

Slovic, P., and Lichtenstien, S. "Comparison of Bayesian and Regression Approaches to the Study of Information Processing in Judgment." *Organizational Behavior and Human Performance,* 1971, 6, 649-744.

Slovic, P., Fischhoff, B., and Lichtenstein, S. "Behavioral Decision Theory." *Annual Review of Psychology,* 1977, 28, 1-39.

Stahl, M. J., and Harrell, A. M. "Modeling Effort Decisions with Behavioral Decision Theory: Toward an Individual Differences Model of Expectancy Theory." *Organizational Behavior and Human Performance,* 1981, 27, 303-25.

Stahl, M. J., and Harrell, A. M. "Evolution and Validation of a Behavioral Decision Theory Measurement Approach to Achievement, Power, and Affiliation." *Journal of Applied Psychology,* 1982, 67(6), 744-751.

Stahl, M. J., and Zimmerer, T. "Modeling Strategic Acquisition of Policies: A Simulation of Executives Acquisition Decisions." *Academy of Management Journal,* 1984, 27(2), 369-383.

Sullivan, J, and Peterson, R. "Trust in Japanese-American Joint Ventures." *Management International Review,* 1982, 22, 30-40.

PART II

Competitive Strategic Decisions

The purpose of this part of the book is to explore THE strategic business-level question: How do we compete in our chosen business? This dimension of strategy has received increasing, much deserved attention in the last decade thanks partly to fierce global competition.

Chapter 8 opens this part with one of the most important business-level decisions at the heart of Porter's (1980, 1985) models of competitive strategy: How does the firm compete in its chosen market? Are cost leadership and differentiation the only two relevant generic ways to compete at the business level? Executives in both the textile and printing industries pursued focus on specific customers or segments of markets as a viable competitive strategy in addition to cost leadership and differentiation. Focus was more prevalent in smaller firms. Interviews and discussions with Chinese managers and educators during a late 1987 lecture tour in the People's Republic of China highlighted the importance of each of the three business-level competitive strategies as a function of the specific international market.

Chapter 9 examines the questions of which markets to enter, how to enter them and when, from the viewpoint of competitive market entry barriers. Cost advantages and product differentiation advantages of firms already in the market, and the capital requirements for new firms to enter the market, were the three most important market entry barriers in the executives' market entry decisions. Customer switching costs, access to distribution channels and government policy were of lesser importance. The higher the importance placed on the barriers, the higher the corporate performance. Also, the higher the consensus on the barriers, the higher the corporate performance. All these statements are true for both early and late market entry.

Chapter 10 deals with an increasingly important competitive strategic issue in many firms. How do we use information technology as a competitive weapon? Due to advances in information technology and the widespread availability of information technology, this competitive question is no longer relevant just for high technology firms.

CHAPTER 8

Competitive Strategic Decisions: Is Focus a Separate Strategy?

BUSINESS STRATEGY DIMENSIONS

Business-level strategy has been based on a variety of dimensions. For example, stage of the product life cycle has been researched as an important dimension of strategy (Hofer, 1975; Anderson and Zeithaml, 1984). Miller and Friesen's (1977) archetypes provide a multivariate view of strategy. Miles and Snow (1978) based a typology on their "adaptive cycle." Hall (1980) used product differentiation and delivered cost. Porter (1980, 1985) used cost leadership, differentiation and focus as the significant dimensions of strategy.

Within this strategy literature, there are several streams related to two dimensions of strategy. Hofer and Schendel (1978) labeled the two dimensions efficiency and effectiveness, and argued that they are the two fundamental strategies that organizations can pursue. For Hofer and Schendel (1978), efficiency is defined by Drucker's (1954) statement that firms should "do things right"; effectiveness is defined by the statement that firms should "do the right thing." Some of the streams of research that have touched on this dichotomy are listed in Figure 8.1.

To say there are only two strategies a firm can pursue is a simplification of a very complex reality. The question most often addressed is whether all firms pursue one of these two strategies or a combination of both. Some have argued that though both can be pursued, it is difficult and typically only one or the other is pursued (Hall, 1980; Miles and Snow, 1978; Porter,

This chapter was written by Michael J. Stahl and Mark D. Hanna, both of Clemson University, and Don M. Parks of the University of Wyoming. An earlier version of this chapter was presented at the November 1986 National Decision Sciences Institute meeting in Honolulu and published in the *Proceedings*, pp. 1252–1254.

Figure 8.1
Strategic Dimensions

Authors	Strategic Alternatives	
Drucker (1954)	Doing things right	Doing the right things
Miles & Snow (1978)	Defenders	Prospectors
Hofer & Schendel (1978)	Efficiency	Effectiveness
Hall (1980)	Low Delivered Cost	High Differentiation
Day (1981)	Top-Down	Bottom-Up
Porter (1980, 1985)	Cost Leadership	Differentiation

1980, 1985). However, recent studies (Phillips, Chang and Buzzell, 1983; Karnani 1984) argue that differentiation and delivered cost are independent and they are not mutually exclusive. Such an argument would allow the existence of additional dimensions such as focus (Porter, 1980, 1985).

Through this stream of research, there has been a conspicuous lack of discussion regarding Porter's (1980, 1985) focus strategy. Perhaps the rationale for the exclusion of the focus strategy is that it is implicit in cost leadership and differentiation strategies and only refers to the breadth of the chosen market (Parks, 1985).

Though Dess and Davis (1984) included focus in a multivariate study of Porter's (1980) strategies, they were unable to "identify clearly the . . . focus strategy." They stated that focus may be difficult to measure because its dimensions can vary so widely across different organizational settings. Wright (1987) recently clarified the issue by arguing that focus is more relevant for smaller firms.

Examination of Porter's (1980, 1985) focus strategy seems an appropriate next step in this stream of research. If focus is found to be similar in importance, future research should include focus as a dimension equal with cost leadership and differentiation. Therefore, the purpose of this research was to determine if focus should be considered as a separate dimension of business strategy and included in research dealing with cost leadership and differentiation. Definitions of these terms are offered in the next section.

The tests were conducted in two separate industries. Since performance data were available in one industry, correlations among the three strategies and performance were computed.

TEXTILE INDUSTRY

Textile Competitive Strategy Decision Making Exercise

In order to test the research question, a decision making exercise was designed to capture choices among the three alternative strategies. Such an exercise was chosen for a number of reasons.

First, several strategy researchers have suggested that a way to analyze business policy is through a decision making framework (Hatten, 1979; Hofer and Schendel, 1978; Mintzberg, 1978; Shirley, 1982).

Second, the decision modeling methodology has been shown to be immune from social desirability response bias (Arnold and Feldman, 1981; Stahl and Harrell, 1982). Given the lofty connotations to Porter's terms, such immunity is desirable.

Third, it was desirable to capture the notion of tradeoffs. This closely approximated the actual decision situation faced by executives in choosing among strategies, especially in a highly competitive industry in which profit margins had been squeezed so tightly that there were insufficient funds to simultaneously pursue all three strategies. Indeed, Porter (1985) argued that a firm should not pursue all three strategies lest it become "stuck in the middle."

The fourth reason refers to the methodological implications of poor cognitive insight. In their literature reviews, Slovic and Lichtenstein (1971) and Slovic, Fischhoff and Lichtenstein (1977) documented the poor cognitive insight that most decision makers have into their own multiple criteria decision processes. Stahl and Zimmerer (1984) empirically demonstrated poor cognitive insight among executives' strategic decisions. Thus, the methodology of asking executives how they make strategic decisions has limitations.

Fifth, the decision modeling methodology serves as a bridge between laboratory experiments and *ex post facto* field studies. In field studies on the content of business strategies, it is very difficult to find appropriate levels of the variables. Even in the widely cited PIMS studies, researchers are forced to use the contextual variables already available, often suffering decreased construct validity as the data are made to "fit" the model (Chapter 1). On the other hand, the decision modeling methodology is able to specify any context desired while using rigorous experimental designs.

Sixth, the decision modeling methodology can serve as a bridge between content and process strategic management research. It can deal with the content of decisions, as this study does regarding differentiation, cost and focus. Decision modeling can also deal with the process of strategy as top management's decision making is a part of the process of strategic management.

The definitions of Porter's three strategies were listed at the front of the exercise and Porter's (1980) text was cited. On the same page in the introduction, the levels used to describe each strategy were also defined. Figure 8.2 contains the definitions and the level descriptions as listed in the exercise.

Figure 8.2
Definition of Terms in Exercise

The following three terms, which relate to specific products or services, were derived from Porter (1980).

Overall Cost Leadership refers to a firm having the lowest cost of manufacture relative to competitors and is the theme running through the firm's strategy, though quality, service, and other areas cannot be ignored. Examples include Japanese Auto Manufacturers, Texas Instruments, and DuPont.

Differentiation refers to a product or service that is perceived industrywide as being unique. Approaches to differentiating can take many forms: design or brand image (Mercedes in autos); features (Jenn-Air in electric ranges); dealer network (Caterpillar Tractor in construction equipment) or other dimensions, such as technology or customer service. Differentiation does not allow the firm to ignore costs, but rather they are not the primary strategic target.

Focus refers to the targeting of a "particular buyer group, segment of the product line, or geographic market. Although the low cost and differentiation strategies are aimed at achieving their objectives industrywide, the entire focus strategy is built around servicing a particular target very well. For example, Fort Howard Paper focuses on a narrow range of industrial-grade papers, avoiding consumer products vulnerable to advertising battles and rapid introductions of new products. Porter Paint focuses on the professional painter rather than the do-it-yourself market." (Porter, 1980, pp. 38-39).

In this exercise, you will be presented with three levels of each strategy.

For Overall Cost Leadership, the levels relative to competitors
      are:
      Lower Cost (Among the lowest 1/3 in cost position);
      Average Cost (Among the middle 1/3 in cost position); and
      Higher Cost (Among the highest 1/3 in cost position).

For Differentiation, the levels relative to competitors are:
      Less Differentiation (Among the least differentiated 1/3);
      Average Differentiation (Among the middle 1/3 in
      differentiation); and
      More Differentiation (Among the most differentiated 1/3).

For Focus, the levels relative to competitors are:
      Less Focus (Among the least focused 1/3);
      Average Focus (Among the middle 1/3 in focus); and
      More Focus (Among the most focused 1/3).

In order to assess the separate contribution of each of the three strategies and possible interactions among the terms, a full factorial design was employed. With three cues each at three levels, 27 separate cases were employed (3 × 3 × 3). Each case was described as a separate business plan for review. Each plan was reviewed for use in three different industry segments—an industrial fabrics manufacturer, a home fabrics manufacturer, and an apparel manufacturer. These three segments of the textile fabrication industry involve different products for different customers. As such, the structure of the industry and of the exercise allowed three separate tests. Figure 8.3 contains an example of one of the business plans.

Analysis

In order to assess the separate contributions of each of the three strategies, the following regression equation was tested for each of the three industry segments.

$$Y_j = B_1(X_{1j}) + B_2(X_{2j}) + B_3(X_{3j}) + B_4(X_{1j})(X_{2j}) + B_5(X_{1j})(X_{3j})$$
$$+ B_6(X_{2j})(X_{3j}) \tag{8.1}$$

$$j = 1, 2, \ldots, 27$$

Figure 8.3
Business Plan #1

This plan consists of the following strategies relative to competitors:

     LOWER COST
     MORE DIFFERENTIATION
     LESS FOCUS

DECISION A: WITH THE LEVELS OF THESE THREE STRATEGIES IN MIND, indicate the chance you would recommend this plan for an <u>Industrial Fabrics</u> manufacturer.

0% 10%   20%   30%   40%   50%   60%   70%   80%   90%   100%

DECISION B: WITH THE LEVELS OF THESE THREE STRATEGIES IN MIND, indicate the chance you would recommend this plan for a <u>Home Fabrics</u> Manufacturer.

0%   10%   20%   30%   40%   50%   60%   70%   80%   90%   100%

DECISION C: WITH THE LEVELS OF THESE THREE STRATEGIES IN MIND, indicate the chance you would recommend this plan for an <u>Apparel</u> Manufacturer.

0%   10%   20%   30%   40%   50%   60%   70%   80%   90%   100%

Where

Y_j = value of decision;

B_1 = standardized regression coefficient or importance attributed to Cost;

X_{1j} = Cost for Business Plan j;

B_2 = standardized regression coefficient or importance attributed to Differentiation;

X_{2j} = Differentiation for Business Plan j;

B_3 = standardized regression coefficient or importance attributed to Focus;

X_{3j} = Focus for Business Plan j.

Equation (8.1) was estimated for the 27 values of Decision A (industrial fabrics), then the 27 values of Decision B (home fabrics), and then the 27 values of Decision C (apparel). Based upon the literature on decision modeling (Slovic and Lichtenstein, 1971; Slovic, Fischhoff, and Lichtenstein, 1977), few interactions were expected. In the case of a lack of significant interactions, the regression models were computed again without the interactions as in Equation (8.2).

$$Y_j = B_1(X_{1j}) + B_2(X_{2j}) + B_3(X_{3j}) \tag{8.2}$$

An advantage to equation (8.2) and an orthogonal design is that the relative contribution of each strategy can be computed as a relative weight through the transformation listed in equation (1.2) (Hoffman, 1960; Ward, 1962).

The Sampled Textile Executives

The exercise was completed by 35 executives in the textile industry. They were department managers, plant managers, general managers or group managers. They completed the exercise as part of a professional development course they were attending at a southeastern university. Given that they were all in the highly competitive textile industry which had recently been battered by foreign textiles, they were extremely interested in the exercise concerning competitive strategy.

Results

The first step in the analysis was to test for the presence of interactions via equation (8.1). Of the 315 possible interactions (3 interactions per equation x 3 equations per subject x 35 subjects), only 3 were found to be significant at the .01 level. There was no pattern to the three interactions. Additionally, interactions in the group models were also tested by calculating equation (8.1) with the Decision A values for all 35 subjects (945 decisions),

Table 8.1
Average Individual Relative Weights (Textile Industry)

Strategy	Industrial	Home	Apparel
Cost	51	41	41
Differentiation	21	30	32
Focus	28	29	27

Note: n = 35 for each of the three industry segments.

then for all Decision B values (945 decisions), and then all Decision C values (945 decisions). In the three group models, none of the nine possible interaction terms were statistically significant. Therefore, the remainder of the analysis was performed with equations (8.2) and (1.2) to assess the main effect terms.

Table 8.1 contains the average individual relative weights from the 105 regression equations. Three separate means tests were conducted to determine if the average relative weights on focus were significantly greater than 0.0. In each of the three industrial segments tested (industrial, home, and apparel), the average individual relative weight on focus was significantly greater than 0.0 (t = 5.58, 7.16, 7.36, respectively; all p < .01). The subjects perceived focus as a separate strategy worthy of consideration.

Means tests were then conducted among the three strategies within the three industrial segments. A Duncan's Multiple Range Test indicated that the average weight on cost was significantly higher than on both focus and differentiation in the industrial segment. Similarly, the average weight on cost was significantly higher than the average weight on focus in the apparel segment. No differences were found among segments within a strategy.

Next, the group models were tested. Table 8.2 contains the results of the three group regression models. Each model was computed by grouping all the decisions for that industrial segment into one regression equation.

Three separate tests on the regression coefficients associated with focus as a strategy were performed to determine if the coefficients were significantly greater than zero. In each of the three tests, the coefficients were found to be greater than zero (t = 11.89, 12.67, and 11.17 for industrial, home, and apparel, respectively; all p < .01). Thus, the subjects were placing significant weight on focus as a strategy as indicated in the individual analyses.

The group regressions were then compared to each other with three Chow's F tests to test for differences among the strategies as a function of industrial segment. The three separate equations were found to be different from one another. Industrial was different from home (F = 5.15, p < .01); industrial was different from apparel (F = 7.48, p < .01); and, home was

Table 8.2
Group Relative Weights (Textile Industry)

Strategy	Industrial	Home	Apparel
Cost	58	45	48
Differentiation	13	30	33
Focus	29	25	19

Note: n = 945 decisions for each of the three industry segments.

different from apparel (F = 3.17, p < .05). As in the individual analyses, this indicated that the subjects had industrial segment specific policies.

PRINTING INDUSTRY
Printing Competitive Strategy Decision Making Exercise

An exercise nearly identical to that discussed for the textile industry was used. Indeed, the same sheet of definitions as shown in Figure 8.2 for the textile industry was used. The same full factorial experimental design of three cues each at three levels for a total of 27 cases (3 × 3 × 3) was also used. The only major difference is that there was only one decision scale for the printing industry unlike Figure 8.3 which contains three decision scales for the textile industry.

In addition to the decisions, the executives were asked to indicate their firm's performance relative to other firms in their industry. A three-point scale was used with possible answers including above, about the same, and below.

The Sampled Printing Managers

The marketing managers of 13 printing firms completed the decision making exercise. Their names were obtained from the Gravure Technical Association, which is a printing industry trade association. Sixty-two other members of GTA chose not to respond to the mailed exercise.

Results

Using equation (8.1) and the individual models, it was found that of the 39 possible interactions (3 interactions per subject x 13 subjects) only one was significant at the .01 level. Using the group model with 351 decisions (27 decisions per subject x 13 subjects), none of the three possible interaction terms were significant. Therefore, the remainder of the analysis was performed with equations (8.2) and (1.2) to assess the main effect terms.

Table 8.3
Relative Weights (Printing Industry)

Strategy	Average Individual	Group
Cost	35	25
Differentiation	31	42
Focus	34	33

Note. n = 13 for the average individual relative weights. For the group regression, 351 decisions were used.

Table 8.3 contains the average individual relative weights from the 13 individual regressions and the relative weights from the group regression. A means test was conducted to determine if the average individual relative weight on focus was significantly greater then 0.0. A t value of 5.66 ($p < .01$) indicated that the weight on focus was greater than 0.0. The regression coefficient on focus from the group model was also tested to determine if it was greater than 0.0. A t value of 4.23 ($p < .01$) indicated that the group value on focus was greater than 0.0. Thus, the subjects were placing significant weight on focus as a strategy as indicated in both analyses.

Means tests were then conducted among the three strategies. A Duncan's Multiple Range Test indicated that there was no significant difference among the average weights placed on cost, differentiation and focus.

The relative weights on the three strategies from the 13 regressions were correlated with the reported performance data. A positive correlation between cost leadership and performance was observed ($r = 0.62$, $p < .05$). Performance displayed two non-significant correlations with differentiation and focus.

COMPARISON BETWEEN INDUSTRIES

To test Wright's (1987) proposition that focus is more relevant for smaller firms, the weight placed on focus by the printing executives was compared to the weight placed on focus by the textile executives. The printing executives represented smaller companies, many with less than 100 employees. The textile executives were from larger companies, many with more than 10,000 employees. Wright's (1987) proposition was supported as the weight placed on focus by the printing executives was greater than the weight placed on focus by the textile executives ($p < .01$).

DISCUSSION AND CONCLUSION

The purpose of this research was to determine if the strategy of focus, as described by Porter (1980, 1985), is a separate and equally important dimension of strategy. Based on the decisions of 35 managers in the textile industry concerning the use of cost leadership, differentiation and focus as strategies in the industrial, home, and apparel segments of the textile industry, it is concluded that focus was employed as a separate strategy. Both individual and group analyses supported that conclusion.

Both individual and group analyses of 13 executives in the printing industry supported the same conclusion: focus was used as a separate strategy. Although focus was supported as a separate strategy, cost leadership as a strategy displayed a significant correlation with firm performance.

Figure 8.1 indicates a lack of agreement among theorists concerning the appropriate treatment of focus as a strategy. The data in this chapter from two different sets of executives in two different industries with two slightly different decision making instruments indicate that focus is used as a separate and important dimension of strategy. The support of Wright's (1987) proposition, which hypothesized that focus is more relevant for smaller firms, lends validity to this research.

The decision modeling methodology employed herein is amenable for use in other industries. Indeed, one need only change the wording on the decision scale to replicate this research in another industry. Perhaps the most significant contribution of this research is the demonstration of a methodology that can serve as a bridge between lab experiment and field study, as well as a bridge between content and process strategic management research.

This research also provides evidence that focus is a dimension of similar significance with differentation and cost leadership. Therefore, focus should be included with them in future studies of business-level strategy.

Postscript on Competitive Strategy

A three-week lecture tour in the People's Republic of China by this book's author in late 1987 highlighted the importance of the three different competitive strategies as a function of the specific market. Interviews, lectures and discussions were held with many Chinese managers and educators in Beijing, Shanghai and Wuxi on competition in the worldwide textile market.

The Chinese interviewed had a good appreciation of cost leadership as a competitive strategy. Indeed, since the lectures were at the China Textile University in Shanghai and the Wuxi Textile Management College, many had experience in the fiercely cost-competitive textile industry. Their extremely low wage rates of about $0.25 (American) per hour afforded them a definite low-cost competitive advantage in non-differentiated textiles, or other industries with standardized products.

There was some understanding of differentiation on the basis of quality as a competitive strategy. Little understanding was evident of differentiation on the basis of style, features, brand identification, or other bases. With their cultural and geographic distances from American markets, competition would be difficult on the basis of style in apparel, or in other markets for which style is important.

Given a lack of understanding of market niches and marketing segments, focus as a competitive strategy did not hold strong appeal for them. Due to this lack of understanding and distance from the Western market niches, the Chinese have handicaps in competing on the basis of focus.

These patterns present some competitive opportunities and threats for American firms who are competing in an increasingly competitive international marketplace. Although American firms cannot match such low wage rates, they should be able to compete successfully on the twin bases of differentiation and focus.

REFERENCES

Anderson, Carl R., and Zeithaml, Carl P. "Stage of the Product Life Cycle, Business Strategy, and Business Performance." *Academy of Management Journal*, 1984, 1, 5–24.

Arnold, H. J., and Feldman, D. C. "Social Desirability Response Bias in Self-Report Choice Situations." *Academy of Management Journal*, 1981, 24, 377–385.

Ashton, R. H. "An Experimental Study of Internal Control Judgments." *Journal of Accounting Research*, 1974, 4, 143–158.

Christoph, R. T., and Stahl, M. J. "Modeling Corporate Divestiture Decisions to Test the Capital Asset Pricing Model." *Proceedings*, National American Institute for Decision Sciences, Las Vegas, November 1985, 689–691.

Darlington, R. B. "Multiple Regression in Psychological Research and Practice." *Psychological Bulletin*, 1968, 69(3), 161–182.

Dawes, R. M., and Corrigan, B. "Linear Models in Decision Making." *Psychological Bulletin*, 1974, 81(2), 95–106.

Day, George S. "Strategic Market Analysis and Definition." *Strategic Management Journal*, 1981, 2, 281–299.

Dess, G. G., and Davis, P. S. "Porter's (1980) Generic Strategies as Determinants of Strategic Group Membership and Organizational Performance." *Academy of Management Journal*, 1984, 27, 467–488.

Drucker, Peter. *The Practice of Management*. New York: Harper and Row, 1954.

Einhorn, J. J., and Hogarth, R. M. "Behavioral Decision Theory: Processes of Judgment and Choice." *Annual Review of Psychology*, 1981, 32, 53–88.

Goldberg, L. H. "Simple Models or Simple Processes? Some Research on Clinical Judgments." *American Psychologist*, 1968, 23, 483–496.

Hall, William K. "Survival Strategies in a Hostile Environment." *Harvard Business Review*, 1980, 58, 75–85.

Hammond, K. R. et al. "Social Judgment Theory: Applications in Policy Formation." In M. F. Kaplan and S. Schwartz, eds. *Human Judgment and Decision Processes in Applied Settings*. New York: Academic Press, 1977, 1–30.

Hatten, K. "Quantitative Research Methods in Strategic Management." In D. E. Schendel and C. W. Hofer, eds. *Strategic Management: A New View of Business Policy and Planning.* Boston: Little, Brown, 1979, 448–466.

Hofer, Charles W. "Toward a Contingency Theory of Business Strategy." *Academy of Management Journal,* 1975, 18, 784–810.

Hofer, C. W. "Research on Strategic Planning: A Survey of Past Studies and Suggestions for Future Efforts." *Journal of Economics and Business,* 1976, 28, 261–286.

Hofer, C. W., and Schendel, D. *Strategy Formulation: Analytical Concepts.* St. Paul: West Publishing, 1978.

Hoffman, P. J. "The Paramorphic Representation of Clinical Judgment." Psychological Bulletin, 1960, 57(2), 116–132.

Kaplan, M. F., and Schwartz, S., eds. *Human Judgment and Decision Processes.* New York: Academic Press, 1975.

Karnani, A. "Generic Competitive Strategies." *Strategic Management Journal,* 1984, 5, 367–380.

Miles, Raymond E., and Snow, Charles. *Organizational Strategy, Structure, and Process.* New York: McGraw-Hill, 1978.

Miles, Raymond E., Snow, Charles C., and Pfeffer, Jeffrey. "Organization Environment: Concepts and Issues." *Industrial Relations,* 1978, 13, 244–264.

Miller, Danny, and Friesen, Peter H. "Strategy Making in Context: Ten Empirical Archetypes." *The Journal of Management Studies,* 1977, 253–280.

Mintzberg, H. "Patterns in Strategy Formation." *Management Sciences,* 1978, 24, 934–948.

Parks, D. M. "An Empirical Examination of the Relationship Between the Strategic Typologies Proposed by Miles and Snow, Porter and Hall." *Proceedings,* Southern Management Association, Orlando, Florida, November 1985.

Phillips, L. W., Chang, D. R., and Buzzell, R. D. "Product Quality, Cost Position and Business Performance: A Test of Some Key Hypotheses." *Journal of Marketing,* 1983, 47(2), 26–43.

Porter, M. E. *Competitive Strategy.* New York: Free Press, 1980.

Porter, M. E. *Competitive Advantage.* New York: Free Press, 1985.

Shirley, R. C. "Limiting the Scope of Strategy: A Decision Based Approach." *Academy of Management Review,* 1982, 7, 262–268.

Slovic, P., and Lichtenstein, S. "Comparison of Bayesian and Regression Approaches to the Study of Information Processing in Judgment." *Organizational Behavior and Human Performance,* 1971, 6, 649–744.

Slovic, P., Fischhoff, B., and Lichtenstein, S. "Behavioral Decision Theory." *Annual Review of Psychology,* 1977, 28, 1–39.

Stahl, M. J., and Harrell, A. M. "Evolution and Validation of a Behavioral Decision Theory Measurement Approach to Achievement, Power and Afiliation." *Journal of Applied Psychology,* 1982, 67, 744–750.

Stahl, M. J., and Zimmerer, T. "Modeling Strategic Acquisition Policies: A Simulation of Executives' Acquisition Decisions." *Academy of Management Journal,* 1984, 27, 369–383.

Ward, J. "Comments on 'The Paramorphic Representation of Clinical Judgment.'" *Psychological Bulletin,* 1962, 59, 74–76.

Wright, P. "A Refinement of Porter's Strategies." *Strategic Management Journal,* 1987, 8, 93–101.

CHAPTER 9

Market Entry Barriers and Market Entry Decisions

BARRIERS TO MARKET ENTRY

Often many firms enter new or familiar markets in an attempt to grow by introducing new or modified products. Alternatively, some firms enter markets with products that are identical to the products already in the market. These firms face market entry barriers and the firms are at great financial risk. The reasons for entry vary, but most firms enter markets to increase market shares or to diversify into new businesses.

Barriers to market entry are crucial environmental factors that influence firms' market shares and profits already in the market. In markets where strong barriers to entry exist, firms have difficulty in entering the markets early or they enter the market as late entrants. Late market entry is usually disadvantageous. However, sometimes it provides some benefits such as entering the market with improved or more technologically advanced products, and not needing to create primary demand for the products.

Yip (1982) defines market entry as the beginning of activities in a market new to the entrant. Barriers to entry are described by Shepherd (1979) as anything that decreases the likelihood, scope, or speed of the potential competitors' coming into the market. Similarly, Porter defines entry barriers as "features of an industry that give incumbents inherent advantages over potential entrants" (1980a, p. 125). Barriers embrace all manner of specific legal devices, such as patents, mineral rights and franchises, as well as more general economic barriers.

Many researchers have stressed the importance of barriers to market entry and have proposed that numerous entry barriers exist. However, they

This chapter was written by Fahri Karakaya of Southeastern Massachusetts University and Michael J. Stahl.

have presented very little empirical support for their proposals. Do market entry barriers influence market entry decision makers? Which entry barriers play the most important role in deterring businesses from entering markets? Do the market entry barriers influence market entrants to make early or late market entry decisions? Is there a relationship between the importance of market entry barriers and firm profitability? Is there a relationship between consensus on the importance of market entry barriers and firm profitability?

This research is aimed at finding answers to the above questions through testing the six major barriers to entry proposals made by Porter (1980b). Porter's entry barrier proposals were chosen because they include the most important entry barriers that have been discussed in previous literature. Porter's entry barriers include the following (1980b, p. 7):

1. Cost advantages of the incumbents
2. Capital requirements
3. Product differentiation
4. Customer switching costs
5. Access to distribution channels
6. Government policy

MARKET ENTRY BARRIERS TESTED

Cost Advantages of Incumbents

Economies of scale and experience curve/learning curve are the two major sources of cost advantages which serve as market entry barriers if used appropriately. The other cost advantages may include those that cannot be copied by potential entrants and serve as market entry barriers. Porter (1980b) indicated that these cost advantages are: (1) proprietary product technology; (2) favorable access to raw materials; (3) favorable location; and (4) government subsidies.

Capital Requirements

Capital requirements is a traditional form of economic market entry barrier which was first delineated by Bain (1956). Porter (1980b) states that the need to invest large financial resources in order to compete creates a barrier to market entry, whether those resources must be raised in capital markets or not.

Harrigan (1981) argues that high capital intensity discourages entry, other factors being held constant. Furthermore, Harrigan claims that if the capital requirements for market entry are high, the likelihood of entry will be lower and the technological scale will be higher.

Eaton and Lipsey (1980) studied the strategic use of capital by firms to create market entry barriers. These researchers concluded that durability of capital acted as a barrier to market entry in certain markets.

Product Differentiation

Product differentiation was first regarded as a market entry barrier by Bain (1956, 1962). Porter (1980b) also considers product differentiation a market entry barrier. According to Porter, product differentiation means that established firms have brand identification and customer loyalties stemming from past advertising, customer service and product differences or simply being first into the industry. In addition, Porter (1985) pointed out that technological changes also play an important role in the pattern of product differentiation.

According to Schmalensee (1982), early market entrants gain product differentiation advantage over later entrants when customers become convinced that the first brand in any product class performs satisfactorily. Then the first brand becomes the standard against which subsequent entrants are rationally judged. Therefore, it becomes harder for later entrants to convince consumers to invest in learning about their products than for the first brand.

Hofer and Schendel present a different view in product differentiation. They claim that "product differentiation is aimed primarily at existing competitors, not at unknown potential entrants" (1978, p. 138). If this is true, then product differentiation cannot act as a strong market entry barrier. Even though firms may not aim their product differentiation strategies at unknown potential entrants, they can still differentiate their products by simply being first into the market (Porter, 1980b; Robinson and Fornell, 1985).

Customer Switching Costs

According to Porter (1980b), switching costs lock the buyer to particular sellers. Usually, technological changes can raise or lower these costs. Porter argues that there are six major sources of switching costs:

1. Cost of modifying a product to match a new supplier's product
2. Cost of testing or certifying a new supplier's product to insure substitutability
3. Investment required in new accessory equipment necessary to use a new supplier's product
4. Investment in retraining employees
5. Cost of establishing new logistical arrangements
6. Psychic cost of severing a relationship with present suppliers

McFarlan (1984) provides a good example of customer switching costs as a market entry barrier. He argues that information technology in most organizations has been used for support function. However, information technology can be used to achieve competitive advantage such as building market entry barriers if the service provided cannot be easily reproduced by competitors. Further, he stresses that customers may be reluctant to switch to a competitor's service if the costs of switching are too high.

Access to Distribution Channels

This market entry barrier has been neglected by researchers despite the fact that it might be a very important one. Unless firms can develop their own distribution channels or acquire other firms to employ as their distributors (that is, vertical integration), access to distribution channels remains an important barrier to market entry. Oftentimes, the first or early entrants use intensive distribution strategies to limit the access to distributors for the potential market entrants.

Porter (1980b) stated that a barrier to market entry can be created by the new entrant's need to secure distribution channels for its product. In addition, Porter (1985) determined that technological change can influence access to distribution by allowing firms to bypass existing channels, or conversely, by increasing industry dependence on channels.

Government Policy

Government policy can easily limit the number of firms in a market through licensing requirements and other controls (Porter, 1980b). Although limiting the number of firms in an industry usually decreases competition, such controls are often aimed at protecting the public and the environment.

Harrigan (1985) studied the effect of governmental issuance of tradable licenses on the market equilibrium. Her findings indicate that licensing not only affects the number of active firms, but also the types of active firms in a market.

Regulatory reforms have had an important impact on the number of firms in industry and on the number of applications filed before the Interstate Commerce Commission to enter interstate motor carrier markets. Despite the increases in the number, Moore (1978) claims that because the operating authorities (permits) were so narrowly drawn, the entry into the motor carrier industry was limited and competition hindered.

Pustay (1985) empirically compared the impact on entry into the motor carrier industry of the administrative and legislative reforms. His conclusions indicated that the effect of the motor carrier act of 1980 was far broader, impacting entry into markets of all sizes, especially the largest. However, the administrative reforms had the effect of reducing some of the regulatory burdens placed upon carriers.

Recently, the federal product and geographic barriers to entry have been reduced in the banking industry. Modification of the Bank Holding Company Act in 1970, the Depository Institutions Deregulation and Monetary Control Act of 1980, and the Garnst Germain Depository Institutions Act of 1982 are the most recent examples. Beatty, Reim, and Schapperle (1985) tested the predictive accuracy of two alternative theories of the effect of a reduction in barriers to entry on the purchase price/book value ratio of an acquired bank. These researchers' empirical results are consistent with the barriers to entry theory of the effect of regulatory change on the purchase price/book value ratio. Specifically, they found a statistically significant decline in merger premiums which were attributed to the joint effect of a changing market structure in the banking industry and the relaxation of barriers to entry.

TIMING OF MARKET ENTRY AND MARKET ENTRY BARRIERS

Barriers to market entry influence businesses to enter markets early, or late—or never. If the market entry barriers are high, one would expect only a few firms to be in a market. Many firms wait for market entry barriers to disappear, thus causing late market entry. However, if market entry barriers are low, one would expect many firms to enter a market early. Most of the studies dealing with early or late market entries have not yet considered how market entry barriers influence firms to make early or late market entry decisions.

Early Market Entry

Established companies are often not the first firms to enter new markets, even if they have obvious strengths. They frequently enter the markets later. Established firms usually place a higher opportunity cost on capital and they are often ill prepared to take technological and product risks necessary in the early phases of industry development (Porter, 1980b).

To be first in the market with a product often provides definite advantages such as higher market share, higher return on investment (ROI), lower production and marketing costs, and technological leadership. According to Urban et al. (1986), theoretical and empirical analyses suggest that order of entry affects the market share potential of later entries and mediates entrants' positioning, pricing, and advertising strategies. Schmalensee (1982) argues that conventional wisdom in marketing and recent empirical research support the notion that there are important advantages to being an early entrant in some markets. Similarly, Robinson and Fornell (1985) report that order of market entry is a major determinant of market share and that market pioneers possess long-lived advantages in consumer goods businesses.

However, Cooper (1979) found that being first in a market offered no particular advantage after studying 100 new product failures and successes. Similarly, Dillion, Calantore, and Worthing (1979) reached a parallel conclusion in their study of 109 firms that had introduced new products. These two studies used the PIMS data base.

One of the most important benefits of being the "first market entrant" or "market pioneer," as characterized by Schmalensee (1982), is the cost advantage gained by the experience curve concept (Boston Consulting Group,

1970). Market pioneers acquire high market shares (Robinson and Fornell, 1985), and the positive correlation between market share and ROI has long been established (Anderson and Zeithaml, 1984; Buzzell, Gale and Sultan, 1975; Buzzell and Wiersema, 1981; Dalrymple and Parsons, 1980; Gale, 1972; Hax and Majluf, 1983; Macmillan, Hambrick and Day, 1982; Schoeffler, Buzzell and Heany, 1984; Shepherd, 1972; Wakerly, 1984).

Other first mover or early market entrant advantages as stated by Porter (1985) include the following: (1) reputation; (2) preempting a product's positioning; (3) switching costs; (4) channel selection; (5) proprietary learning curve; (6) favorable access to facilities, inputs or other resources; (7) definition of standards; (8) institutional barriers; and (9) early profits. Furthermore, Porter stresses that first movers and early market entrants get the opportunity to define the competitive rules in a variety of areas. Similarly, Smiley and Ravid (1983) suggest that the potential entrants are unlikely to have greater cumulative output than the incumbent or the early entrant, since their attempts to gain market shares through cutting price can be matched immediately by the intitial monopolist. Furthermore, the initial monopolist will lose less than the new entrant in a price war due to the incumbent's first mover advantage.

Dalrymple and Parsons (1980) suggest that a firm is probably better off being first in pickles than third in soup, even though soup is a much bigger market. This statement, of course, suggests that the size of the market is not the most important factor. Although the market size might be small, being first in that market may provide long-lived advantages (that is, high market share). Porter (1980b) states that being first or one of the early entrants can minimize entry costs and also sometimes yield an advantage in product differentiation. Furthermore, simply being a first entrant can yield a favorable product image. Buyers tend to know and favor the pioneering product; they have no reason to experiment with subsequent entries (Schmalensee, 1982).

Bond and Lean (1977, 1979) determined that important and long-lived advantages are enjoyed by pioneering brands of prescription drugs. These advantages can be overcome by later entrants only if they offer distinct therapeutic benefits, not just lower prices.

Most of the above findings are also consistent with the studies conducted by Abel and Hammond (1979), Urban et al. (1986), Whitten (1979), and with the theoretical work of Schmalensee (1982).

First movers and early market entrants have some disadvantages also. As indicated by Porter (1985), these disadvantages include the following: (1) costs, associated with being a marketing pioneer or early entrant which consist of gaining regulatory approvals, achieving code compliance, educating buyers, developing infrastructure in areas such as service facilities and training, investing in the development of complimentary products, and absorbing the high costs of early inputs because of scarcity of supply and small scale of needs; (2) demand uncertainty; (3) changes in buyer needs; (4) specificity of investments to early generation or factor costs; (5) technological discontinuities; and (6) low-cost imitation.

Another major disadvantage of being the first or early entrant is that the first or early entrant must create primary demand for the product when none exists through heavy investment in promotion. However, the competitors find it convenient to piggyback since by the time they enter the market, the primary demand is already there (Jain, 1981). This disadvantage, of course, translates to advantage for followers and late entrants.

Late Market Entry

According to Schnaars (1986), late market entry strategies are usually designed to imitate firms that are forced, by default, to react to the moves of more insightful competitors. Late market entries are often termed "me too" entries and they are unlikely to succeed. However, a well-developed "second-but-better" entry backed by aggressive promotion may be able to surpass the pioneer's entry (Urban et al., 1986).

Later entrants into an industry may tend to be firms with increased financial resources who can afford to wait until some of the uncertainties in the industry are resolved. Firms with few resources, on the other hand, could have been compelled to enter early when capital costs of entry were low (Porter, 1980b).

Levitt (1965) favors late market entry strategy if firms can employ the so-called "used apple" policy: Instead of bearing the burden of pioneering markets, let others enter the market first; if the market turns out to be attractive, then enter the market. Similarly, Glazer (1985) states that later entrants choose to enter only successful markets which have reached an appreciable size. In a later article, Levitt (1966) argues that imitation is more plentiful than innovation, and is a much more popular way to business growth and profits.

Use of appropriate market entry strategies (early or late) often depends on the type of industry. Entering a technically unsophisticated product market is not the same as entering a technically sophisticated product market because of the presence of usually high market entry barriers in the latter. Samli and Wills (1986) suggest seven different successful market entry strategies into high-tech industries, but fail to consider the existence of high market entry barriers in these industries.

In summary, research concerning the relationship between early or late market entry and competitive advantage is inconclusive. There are numerous factors that play important roles in determining the new entrants' successes. The presence or absence of market entry barriers are probably the most important group of strategic variables that contribute to the successes or failures of early or late entrants.

With the preceding literature review in mind, the following hypotheses were tested in this research:

H1: As market entry barriers, cost advantages, product differentiation, capital requirements, customer switching costs, access to distribution channels, and government policy are not associated with market entry decisions.

H2: There is no difference in importance among the market entry barriers when making market entry decisions.

H3: Market entry barriers are not important in influencing the market entrants to make early or late market entry decisions in consumer goods markets.

H4: There is no relationship between the importance of market entry barriers as perceived by respondents and firms' profitability.

H5: There is no relationship between consensus on the importance of market entry barriers as perceived by respondents and firms' profitability.

RESEARCH METHODOLOGY

The Sampled Marketing Managers

The data for the purpose of this study were gathered through a decision making exercise mailed to executive members of the American Marketing Association (AMA). Sixty major U.S. companies were selected from the AMA directory based on the number of AMA members per company. The companies selected were those with 12 or more members. The purpose of this procedure was to receive multiple responses from each company. Multiple responses were needed to test hypotheses 4 and 5. Responses were received from 139 individuals and 137 of them were fully usable.

The Market Entry Exercise

A decision making exercise was used for three reasons. First, multiple criteria are involved in a decision to enter a market. Thus, it is necessary to simultaneously consider the multiple criteria, versus independently considering each criteria. Second, the amount of information the decision makers use in making decisions can be controlled. This allows a rigorous test of early and late market entry decisions. Third, the decision modeling methodology has been shown to be immune from social desirability response bias (Arnold and Feldman, 1981). Given the lofty connotations of some market entry barriers, like cost advantage and product differentiation, such immunity is desirable.

The exercise was designed around a one-half replicate of a full factorial design with the six criteria each at two levels. This yielded 32 market entry conditions ($1/2 \times 2 \times 2 \times 2 \times 2 \times 2 \times 2$). Since both early and late market entry were tested for both consumer and industrial goods, 4 decisions for each of the 32 conditions were required. This yielded a total of 128 entry decisions per subject. However, only the market entry decisions into consumer goods market are described in this chapter. Figure 9.1 contains an example from the market entry decision making exercise.

Figure 9.1
Sample Market Condition

```
                    MARKET CONDITION

     .  Cost Advantages of Incumbents..................Low
     .  Product Differentiation of Incumbents..........High
     .  Capital Requirements to enter market...........Low
     .  Customer Switching Cost........................Low
     .  Access to Distribution Channels................Low
     .  Government Policy..............................Low
```

With the level of these 6 market entry barriers in mind, indicate the chance you would recommend market entry (please circle the percentages)...

...<u>Decision A</u>: If the above represents an early market entry opportunity into Consumer Goods Market.

No Chance 0%   10%   20%   30%   40%   50%   60%   70%   80%   90%   100%   Definite

...<u>Decision B</u>: If the above represents a late market entry opportunity into Consumer Goods Market.

No Chance 0%   10%   20%   30%   40%   50%   60%   70%   80%   90%   100%   Definite

...<u>Decision C</u>: If the above represents an early market entry opportunity into Industrial Goods Market.

No Chance 0%   10%   20%   30%   40%   50%   60%   70%   80%   90%   100%   Definite

...<u>Decision D</u>: If the above represents a late market entry opportunity into Industrial Goods Market.

No Chance 0%   10%   20%   30%   40%   50%   60%   70%   80%   90%   100%   Definite

---

RESULTS

The data were first analyzed by examining the internal consistency of the decision makers. This was accomplished through inspection of R^2 resulting from the individual regressions on the six main effects. The mean R^2 for Decision A was 0.76, and for decision B was 0.71. All 137 individuals had significant R^2, that is, greater than 0.38.

The statistical significance of the interaction terms was also examined. A model consisting of the 6 main effects and the 15 possible two-way interactions was analyzed at the individual and group level. The model was computed with Decision A as the dependent variable. The model was then recomputed with Decision B as the dependent variable. Significant standardized beta coefficients at the $\alpha = 0.01$ level were noted. The two-way interaction terms were only statistically significant for a very small percent of the respondents (4 percent for early and 5 percent for late market entry decisions). Therefore, the remainder of the analysis is based upon the main effects only.

Table 9.1
Means Test of Relative Weights for Market Entry Barriers

Decision Cues[a]	Early Entry		Late Entry	
	Mean	t*	Mean	t*
CAI	.209	16.12	.218	15.28
PDI	.196	13.63	.194	13.59
CR	.205	14.37	.204	13.75
CSC	.131	13.54	.149	12.72
ADC	.141	11.48	.128	10.46
GP	.118	9.22	.107	9.02

Note: n=137.

*All Market Entry Barriers are statistically different from zero (p<0.01) using t-tests.

a.   CAI = Cost Advantages of Incumbents
     PDI = Product Differentiation of Incumbents
     CR = Capital Requirements
     CSC = Customer Switching Costs
     ADC = Access to Distribution Channels
     GP = Government Policy

Hypothesis 1

The statistical significance of the six market entry barriers was tested by conducting t-tests. The results for each market entry decision are presented in Table 9.1. The null hypothesis is rejected at the $\alpha = 0.01$ level supporting Porter's (1980b) propositions that cost advantages of incumbents, product differentiation of incumbents, capital requirements to enter market(s), customer switching costs, access to distribution channels, and government policy are perceived as barriers to market entry. This condition is true for both decisions, early and late market entry into consumer goods markets.

Hypothesis 2

The difference in importance among the market entry barriers was determined by investigating the relative weights associated with each market entry barrier for two market entry decisions, early and late market entry. Two one-way analysis of variance (ANOVA) and Duncan's Multiple Range tests were utilized to test this hypothesis.

The ANOVAs comparing relative weights of market entry barriers for two decisions clearly indicate that differences exist among the weights of the given market entry barriers. For early market entry into consumer goods markets, the importance attached to market entry barriers differ significantly ($F_{5,816} = 10.22$, $p < 0.01$). Table 9.2 indicates which market entry barriers are actually different at $p < 0.05$ level. According to Duncan's Multiple Range Test, cost advantages of incumbents, capital requirements to enter market(s) and product differentiation entry barriers are significantly greater than the other three market entry barriers of customer switching costs, access to distribution channels and government policy.

The ANOVA results when making late market entry show that the importance of the market entry barriers significantly differ ($F_{5,816} = 11.61$, $p < 0.01$). Duncan's Multiple Range Test (Table 9.4) also indicates that cost advantages of incumbents, product differentiation and capital requirements barriers are significantly greater than the other three barriers. This pattern

Table 9.2
Duncan's Multiple Range Test for Early Market Entry Decisions

		Relative Weights[b]					
Average Relative Weights[c]		CAI[a]	PDI	CR	CSC	ADC	GP
.209	CAI	-					
.196	PDI	NS	-				
.205	CR	NS	NS	-			
.131	CSC	S	S	S	-		
.141	ADC	S	S	S	NS		
.118	GP	S	S	S	NS	NS	-

a. Decision Cues are defined in Table 9.1.

b. Letter S means the relative weights are significantly different and letter NS means the relative weights are not significantly different at the $\alpha = 0.05$ level using Duncan's Multiple Range Test.

c. n=137.

Table 9.3
Duncan's Multiple Range Test for Late Market Entry Decisions

		Relative Weights[b]					
Average Relative Weights[c]		CAI[a]	PDI	CR	CSC	ADC	GP
.218	CAI	–					
.194	PDI	NS	–				
.204	CR	NS	NS	–			
.149	CSC	S	S	S	–		
.128	ADC	S	S	S	NS		
.107	GP	S	S	S	NS	NS	–

a. Decision Cues are defined in Table 9.1.

b. Letter S means the relative weights are significantly different and letter NS means the relative weights are not significantly different at the $\alpha = 0.05$ level using Duncan's Multiple Range Test.

c. n=137.

is the same as the early market entry decision. In addition, customer switching costs barrier differs from the access to distribution channels barrier.

Hypothesis 3

The hypothesized differences in the influence of market entry barriers when making early or late market entry into consumer goods markets were first examined by performing MANOVA. The MANOVA results were statistically significant (Wilks Lambda = .921, F = 6.810, p<0.01).

Table 9.4 presents the six paired t-tests results. The customer switching costs barrier is the only one that differs for early and late market entry decisions. This barrier is perceived to be more important for late market entry decisions.

Hypothesis 4

Three performance measures (return on assets, return on sales, and firm's relative performance during last fiscal year) were used in the analysis. Data

Table 9.4

Comparison of Market Entry Barrier Relative Weights for Early and Late Entry

Decision Cues[a]	Average Relative Weights Early Entry	Average Relative Weights Late Entry	t
CAI	0.209	0.218	-0.80
PDI	0.196	0.194	0.26
CR	0.205	0.204	0.06
CSC	0.131	0.149	-2.49*
ADC	0.141	0.128	1.57
GP	0.118	0.107	1.53

a. Decision Cues are defined in Table 9.1.

*p<0.01, two tailed, paired sample t-test.

Note: n=137.

for firm's return on assets over five years from 1982 to 1986 and return on sales over the same five years were obtained from the *Value Line Investment Survey* (1987).

Almost all respondents (n = 135) responded to the relative performance question in the instrument. The question was a five-point scale ranging from "Much Better Than Average" to "Far Below Average." There were 33 responding companies that had three or more respondents. The average rating for all respondents within a firm was used. Thus, most of the analysis for this hypothesis was performed on 33 or fewer companies. A Spearman Brown Inter-Rater Reliability Coefficient (Kerlinger, 1973) for the relative performance question in the instrument was also calculated. A reliability coefficient of .84 (for 30 firms and 90 raters) was obtained indicating that the respondents highly agreed on their firms' relative performances.

Correlation coefficients were calculated among the three performance variables of return on assets, return on sales and the average relative performance as reported by the respondents. Return on assets was positively correlated with return on sales and relative performance (r = .82, p <0.01), and (r = .43, p <0.01), respectively. Return on sales was positively correlated with relative performance (r = .39, p <0.05).

Canonical correlation analyses were performed using the relative weights for the six barriers as the predictor linear composite and the three performance measures as the criterion linear composite. For early market entry, the two sets of variables were positively related (Wilks Lambda = .018, F. = 354.533, p<0.01). Similarly, the canonical correlation analysis for late market entry was statistically significant (Wilks Lambda = .016, F = 419.945, p<0.01). The relationship between the two sets of variables indicates that as the importance placed on market entry barriers increases, so does the performance. Simple correlation analyses were also performed between the performance variables and the importance of variables individually. Table 9.5 shows the correlation analyses results for early market entry. The importance of the cost advantages barrier was positively related to relative performance (r = .35, p<0.05). This means that as the importance placed on cost advantages barrier increases, so does the performance.

The relationships between the performance variables and the importance of market entry barriers when making late entry are somewhat similar. Correlation analyses showed that only the relative importance of access to distribution channels barrier was positively related to return on assets (r = .39, p<0.05) and return on sales (r = .34, p<0.05). Table 9.6 shows the correlation coefficients.

Hypothesis 5

The hypothesized relationship between firm performance and consensus among the respondents on the importance of market entry barriers was first

Table 9.5
Correlations of Performance and Market Entry Barriers for Early Market Entry

Average Relative Weights[a]	Return on Assets[b]	Return on Sales[b]	Relative Performance[c]
CAI	-.026	.058	.351**
PDI	-.017	.086	-.030
CR	.030	-.012	.078
CSC	.025	-.020	-.108
ADC	.181	.100	.094
GP	-.162	-.166	-.001

a. Decision cues are defined in Table 9.1. The average relative weights refer to the average of all the respondents within a firm.

b. n=29.

c. n=33.

**p<0.05, one tailed significance.

Table 9.6

Correlations of Performance and Market Entry Barriers for Late Market Entry

Average Relative Weights[a]	Return on Assets[b]	Return on Sales[b]	Relative Performance[c]
CAI	-.104	-.054	.136
PDI	-.060	-.046	.080
CR	-.009	.004	-.130
CSC	-.177	-.158	-.171
ADC	.393**	.343**	.181
GP	-.054	-.134	-.162

a. Decision cues are defined in Table 9.1. The average relative weights refer to the average of all the respondents within a firm.

b. n=29.

c. n=33.

   **p<0.05, one tailed significance.

tested by using canonical correlation analyses similar to hypothesis 4. A composite index was used as a measure of consensus on all barriers. This composite index was obtained by subtracting the average R^2 of the individuals in each company from the group R^2 per company. Unless there is perfect agreement among the individuals per company, the composite index will always be less than zero. Two composite indices were calculated for each firm representing consensus on barriers for early and late entry decisions. Peformance variables and the composite indices were plotted to check for non-linearity. The plots showed no clear pattern of non-linear relationships.

Again, the three performance variables mentioned earlier were used as the criterion linear composite and the two consensus indices were used as the predictor linear composite. Canonical correlation analysis showed that firm performance and the consensus on the importance of barriers for early and late market entry were positively associated (Wilks Lambda = 0.020, F = 393.042, p<0.01). As the agreement on the importance of barriers increased, so did the performance.

Simple correlation analyses were also performed to examine the relationship of consensus and performance variables individually. For early market entry (Table 9.7), consensus on barriers was positively related to return on

Table 9.7

Correlations of Performance and Consensus on Market Entry Barriers

Consensus	Return on Assets[a]	Return on Sales[a]	Relative Performance[b]
Early Entry	.354**	.295	.334**
Late Entry	.347**	.223	.181

a.   n=29.

b.   n=33.

**p<0.05, one tailed significance.

assets (r = .35, p < 0.05) and firm's relative performance (r = .33, p < 0.05). For late market entry, return on assets was related to consensus (r = .35, p < 0.05). The correlation coefficients indicate that as the agreement on the importance of barriers increases, so does the performance.

CONCLUSIONS AND DISCUSSION

Importance of Market Entry Barriers

Evidence gathered in this research supports Porter's (1980b) six barriers to market entry proposals, that is, cost advantages of incumbents, product differentiation of incumbents, capital requirements, customer switching costs, access to distribution channels, and government policy. While the importance of barriers differed, all six barriers were perceived as important factors to consider when making market entry decisions. Therefore, these six barriers deter executive decision makers from entering markets.

Some market entry barriers are clearly more important than others. This is evidenced by the differences in the relative weights associated with the six barriers. The cost advantages of incumbents barrier was perceived as the most critical for both early and late market entry into customer goods markets in this study. This is consistent with the business-level strategy of cost leadership (Porter, 1980b).

The capital requirements barrier follows the cost advantages barrier as the second most important barrier. Similar to capital requirements, capital investment was studied as one of the strategic determinants of firm profitability (Schoeffler, Buzzell and Heany, 1974; Schendel and Patton, 1978). Thus, the importance of this barrier is consistent with previous research.

The product differentiation of incumbents barrier is perceived as the third most important barrier for both market entry decisions. Product differentiation is the second business-level strategy proposed by Porter (1980b). Firms try to differentiate their products to deter other firms from entering markets and increase market shares. It is important to note that this study undoubtedly supports the importance of product differentiation strategy.

The remaining three barriers, customer switching costs, access to distribution channels and government policy, differ in their importance depending on the market entry condition. For early entry into consumer goods markets, access to distribution channels is considered as the fourth most important barrier. This barrier is followed by customer switching costs and the government policy barriers. For late entry into consumer goods markets, customer switching costs gain importance as the fourth most important and is followed by access to distribution channels and the government policy barriers. It is interesting to note that the government policy barrier is considered to be the least important barrier for both market entry decisions.

Differences of Market Entry Barriers for Early and Late Entry

For early and late entry into consumer goods markets, only one barrier is different. Customer switching costs barrier is perceived as more important for late entry into consumer goods markets. The seriousness of customer switching costs for late market entry supports Porter's (1985) suggestion that early market entrants have advantages in customer switching costs.

Importance of Market Entry Barriers and Performance

There is a positive relationship between the overall importance of market entry barriers and the three performance variables used in this study. However, the importance of only a few barriers is related to performance. For early market entry, only the importance of the cost advantages barrier was related to performance. For late market entry, the importance of access to distribution channels was associated with performance.

Relationship between Consensus and Performance

There are positive relationships between consensus on the importance of market entry barriers and corporate performance measured by return on assets and relative performance. For both early and late market entries, consensus on the importance of barriers was related to performance. As agreement among the respondents within a firm on the importance of the six barriers increases, so does firm performance. This finding is consistent with previous research which examined the relationship between consensus and performance (Dess and Origer, 1987).

In conclusion, this study provides empirical support for the market entry proposals made by Porter (1980) and shows that these barriers vary for different market entry decisions. Furthermore, it was determined that the importance attached to barriers differs in each market entry decision. The study also provides support for positive relationships between corporate performance and the importance of barriers, as well as consensus on the importance of barriers and corporate performance.

Future Research

It is important to realize that most of the firms included in this study were considered to be successful and large firms. Therefore, the results obtained from this research are only applicable to large and successful firms. It is equally important to consider the executives of medium and small firms, as well as unsuccessful firms. Comparison of the successful and unsuccessful, large, medium and small firms' market entry decisions in the presence and absence of market entry barriers would contribute greatly to the study of market entry barriers. Future studies could focus on individual industries, as well as a crosssection of industries and examine the differences among different industries.

REFERENCES

Abel, Derek, and Hammond, John S. *Strategic Market Planning*. Englewood Cliffs, N.J.: Prentice-Hall, Inc., 1979.

Anderson, Carl R., and Zeithaml, Carl P. "Stage of the Product Life Cycle, Business Strategy, and Business Peformance." *Academy of Management Journal,* 1984, 27 (1), 5–24.

Arnold, H. J., and Feldman, D. C. "Social Desirability Response Bias in Self-Report Choice Situations." *Academy of Management Journal,* 1981, 24, 377–385.

Bain, J. S. *Barriers to New Competition*. Cambridge, Mass.: Harvard University Press, 1956.

Bain, J. S. *Industrial Organization*. New York: John Wiley & Sons, 1962.

Beatty, Randolph P., Reim, John F., and Schapperle, Robert F. "The Effect of Entry on Bank Shareholder Wealth: Implications for Interstate Banking." *Journal of Banking Research,* 1985, 16, 8–15.

Bond, R. S., and Lean, David F. "Sales Promotion and Product Differentiation in Two Prescription Drug Markets" (1977). In Richard Schmalensee, "Product Differentiation Advantages of Pioneering Brands." *The American Economic Review,* 1982, 72 (3), 350–371.

Bond, R. S., and Lean, David F. "Consumer Preference Advertising and Sales: On the Advantages from Early Entry" (1979). In Richard Schmalensee, "Product Differentiation Advantages of Pioneering Brands." *The American Economic Review,* 1982, 72 (3), 350–371.

Boston Consulting Group. *Perspectives: The Experience Curve Reviewed*. Boston, Mass.: Boston Consulting Group, 1970.

Buzzell, Robert D., and Gale, B. T., and Sultan, R. G. M. "Market Share: A Key to Profitability." *Harvard Business Review*, 1975, 5, 97–106.

Buzzell, Robert D., and Wiersema, Frederick D. "Successful Share-Building Strategy." *Harvard Business Review*, 1981, 59, 135–144.

Cooper, R. G. "The Dimensions of New Product Success and Failure." *Journal of Marketing*, 1979, 43, 93–103.

Dalrymple, Douglas J., and Parsons, Leonard J. *Marketing Management: Text and Cases.* 2d ed. New York: John Wiley & Sons, 1980.

Dess, Gregory G., and Origer, Nancy. "Environment, Structure, and Consensus in Strategy Formulation: A Conceptual Integration." *Academy of Management Review*, 1987, 12, (2), 313–330.

Dillion, William R., Calantore, Roger, and Worthing, Porter. "The New Product Problem: An Approach For Investigating Product Failures." *Management Science*, 1979, 25, 1184–1196.

Eaton, Curtis B., and Lipsey, Richard G. "Exit Barriers and Entry Barriers: The Durability of Capital as a Barrier to Entry." *Bell Journal of Economics*, 1980, 11 (2), 721–729.

Gale, B. T. "Market Share and Return on Investment." *Review of Economics and Statistics*, 1972, 54, 412–423.

Glazer, A. "The Advantages of Being First." *The American Economic Review*, 1985, 75 (3), 473–480.

Harrigan, Kathryn R. "Barriers to Entry and Competitive Strategies." *Strategic Management Journal*, 1981, 2 (4), 395–412.

Harrigan, Kathryn R. "An Application of Clustering for Strategic Group Analysis." *Strategic Management Journal*, 1985, 6, 55–73.

Hax, Arnold C., and Majluf, Nicholas S. "The Use of the Growth-Share Matrix in Strategic Planning." *Interfaces*, 1983, 13 (1), 46–60.

Hofer, Charles W., and Schendel, Dan. *Strategy Formulation: Analytical Concepts.* St. Paul: West Publishing Co., 1978.

Jain, Subhash C. *Marketing Planning and Strategy.* Cincinnati, Ohio: South-Western Publishing Co., 1981.

Kerlinger, Fred N. *Foundations of Behavioral Research*, 2d ed. N.Y.: Holt, Rinehart and Winston, Inc., 1973.

Levitt, Theodore. "Exploit the Product Life Cycle." *Harvard Business Review*, November-December 1965, 81–94.

Levitt, Theodore. "Innovative Imitation." *Harvard Business Review*, September-October 1966, 63.

Macmillan, I. C., Hambrick, D. C., and Day, D. L. "The Product Portfolio and Profitability—A PIMS-Based Analysis of Industrial Product Businesses." *Academy of Management Journal*, 1982, 25, 733–755.

McFarlan, Warren F. "Information Technology Changes The Way You Compete." *Harvard Business Review*, May-June 1984, 98–103.

Moore, Thomas G. "The Beneficiaries of Trucking Regulation." *Journal of Law and Economics*, 1978, 21 (2), 327–334.

Porter, Michael. "Industry Structure and Competitive Strategy: Keys to Profitability." In S. H. Britt, H. W. Boyd, Jr., R. T. Davis, and J. Larreche, eds., *Marketing Management and Administrative Action*. New York: McGraw-Hill, 1980a.

Porter, Michael. *Competitive Strategy.* New York: The Free Press, 1980b.

Porter, Michael. "Technology and Competitive Advantage." *Journal of Business Strategy*, 1985, (3), 60–78.

Pustay, Michael W. "Reform of Entry into Motor Carrier Act of 1980 Necessary?" *Transportation Journal*, 1985, 25, 11–24.

Robinson, William T., and Fornell, Cleas. "Sources of Market Pioneering Advantages in Consumer Goods Industries." *Journal of Marketing Research*, 1985, 305–317.

Samli, Coskun, and Wills, James. "Strategies for Marketing Computers and Related Products." *Industrial Marketing Management*, 1986, 15, 23–32.

Schendel, D., and Patton, G. "A Simultaneous Equation Model of Corporate Strategy." *Management Science*, 1978, 24, 1611–1621.

Schmalensee, Richard. "Product Differentiation Advantages of Pioneering Brands." *The American Economic Review*, 1982, 72 (3), 350–371.

Schnaars, Stephen P. "When Entering Growth Markets, Are Pioneers Better than Poachers?" *Business Horizons*, March-April 1986, 27–36.

Schoeffler, Sidney, Buzzell, Robert D., and Heany, Donald F. "Impact of Strategic Planning on Profit Performance." *Harvard Business Review*, 1974, 52, 137–145.

Shepherd, W. "The Elements of Market Structure." *Review of Economics and Statistics*, February 1972, 25–37.

Shepherd, W. *The Economies of Industrial Organization*. Englewood Cliffs, N.J.: Prentice-Hall, 1979.

Smiley, Robert H., and Ravid, S. Abraham. "The Importance of Being First: Learning Price and Strategy." *The Quarterly Journal of Economics*, May 1983, 353–362.

Urban, Glen L. et al. "Market Share Rewards to Pioneering Brands: An Empirical Analysis and Strategic Implications." *Management Science*, 1986, 32 (6), 645–659.

Wakerly, R. G. "PIMS: A Tool for Developing Competitive Strategy." *Long Range Planning*, 1984, 17, 92–97.

Whitten, I. T. "Brand Performance in the Cigarette Industry and the Advantage to Early Entry, 1913–1974" (1979). In Glen L. Urban, Theresa Carter, and Zofia Mucha, "Market Share Rewards to Pioneering Brands: An Empirical Analysis and Strategies Applications." *Working Paper* No. 1454-83, Alfred P. Sloan School of Management, Massachusetts Institute of Technology, 1983.

Yip, G. S. *Barriers to Entry: A Corporate Strategy Perspective*. Lexington, Mass.: D. C. Heath and Company, 1982.

CHAPTER 10

Information Strategy as a Competitive Weapon

During the last two decades, many firms have used information systems (IS) technology to gain a competitive advantage within their respective industries. The decision to invest in an IS project is a critical decision that oftentimes determines the long-term profitability of a firm within an industry and whether a firm will outperform competitors in the industry. Ideally, the selection of an IS technology project would evolve from the overall corporate strategy. There must be a clear integration between the selection of an IS project and the company's strategy. Unfortunately, communications between top management and management information systems (MIS) personnel are oftentimes poor. To further complicate the situation, IS technology projects that offer the potential for competitive advantage are usually risky, long-term commitments (Buday, 1987).

The current management literature is replete with examples linking information technology to a firm's strategy (Cash and Konsynski, 1985; Lucas, 1982; McFarlan, 1981; McFarlan, McKenney, and Pyburn, 1983; Parsons, 1983; Porter and Millar, 1985). Titles such as "IS Redraws Competitive Boundaries" (Cash and Konsynski, 1985); "Information Technology Changes the Way You Compete" (McFarlan, 1984); "Information Technology: A New Competitive Weapon" (Parsons, 1983); "How Information Technology Gives You Competitive Advantage" (Porter and Millar, 1985) are indicative of this trend.

Why has there been so much interest in the integration of information systems technology with strategy during the last five years? Alan Kantrow notes that "this link exists because technology defines the range of possibilities and oftentimes provides the means of implementing the

This chapter was written by Judy D. Holmes of Clemson University and Michael J. Stahl.

strategy. . . . A critical link between technology and strategy exists, the only real choice is whether managers want to see it" (Kantrow, 1980, p. 7).

Although operations research literature has dealt extensively with the topic of research and development (R&D) project selection, little attention has been given to the selection of IS technology projects. This chapter uses policy capturing to model the decision making process of managers who influence the selection of IS projects. Several factors or cues (return on investments, risk, competitive advantage potential and cost of the IS project) that may influence managers as they decide whether to invest in an IS are evaluated.

PURPOSE OF THE STUDY

The purpose of this research is twofold. First, this research examines the relative importance (the weights) that decision makers place on cost, risk, competitive advantage potential, and return on investment as they evaluate IS technology projects. Second, this research addresses the question "Do managers who have successfully utilized IS technology to gain a competitive advantage place less weight on cost, return on investment, and risk than other managers in the same industry?"

EXAMPLES OF FIRMS USING IS TECHNOLOGY FOR A COMPETITIVE EDGE

Perhaps the impetus for the surge of interest in the integration of IS technology and strategy exists due to companies who have successfully accomplished this integration. Examples of companies that have been able to gain a competitive advantage using IS technology are numerous. However, Michael Porter argues that all have gained this competitive edge due to increasing product differentiation or improving cost position. Porter states that "technology affects competitive advantage if it has a significant role in determining relative cost position or differentiation" (Porter, 1985, p. 169). Following are examples of both situations.

American Airlines

An often-cited example of a company gaining a competitive advantage through differentiation achieved with IS technology is American Airlines' Sabre reservation system. American started designing Sabre when United Airlines, Inc. announced plans for its own reservation system for travel agents. United's system was just for its own flights. American made the decision to provide all airlines' schedules so that agents would use their system all the time. By creating total dependence on its system, American Airlines gained market share. It listed its own flights first and many agents never looked further. Max Hooper, executive vice-president of American

Airlines, recently stated "we saw it as a marketing tool from day one" (Harris, 1985, p. 110). American Airlines leases reservations and ticketing terminals to travel agents. The Sabre reservation system has allowed American Airlines to gain a competitive advantage through differentiation of its services. It is interesting to note that the Sabre reservation system is used within American Airlines for ticketing and issuing boarding passes as well as inroute scheduling. Thus, an interdependence of IS technology exists in American Airlines' Sabre reservation system (Porter, 1985).

American Hospital Supply Company

A classic example of a company gaining a competitive edge using IS technology to reduce its relative cost position is provided by American Hospital Supply Company (AHSC). AHSC customers consist of purchasing agents for hospitals and clinics. A market survey revealed that AHSC's current and potential customers wanted a central distributor of medical supplies that could meet most of a hospital's needs. AHSC decided to implement a full-line product distribution strategy. A computer terminal was placed in each customer's office. AHSC's system did order entry, invoicing and billing, inventory control and shipping—automatically and with a high degree of timeliness, responsiveness and accuracy. This supply company could now meet a 24-hour delivery schedule. Thus, customers were able to reduce their inventory stock levels from 75 to 30 days and the customers' purchasing and inventory financing costs went down. Since 1978 when AHSC embarked on this strategy, its sales have grown at an approximate compounded rate of 17 percent per year. It enjoys pre-tax profit margins about four times the industry average and a market share of nearly 50 percent (McFarlan, 1984).

Avis

Another example of a company using IS technology to reduce its relative cost position is Avis car rental. Avis car rental uses the Wizard system to improve its service to customers. Wizard provides Avis with information about the location, cost and performance of its fleet, which helps Avis bargain more effectively with its suppliers. Thus, Avis gained a competitive advantage over Hertz, National and other car rental agencies. "The national network and the service levels it established 'uped the ante' for getting into the business and served as a barrier to entry" (Janulaitis, 1984). In addition, Wizard improved the cost/performance ratios and forestalled the development of substitutes.

Did these companies achieve this competitive edge through luck? Is there some conceptual process or framework that can be utilized to translate IS technology into corporate strategy? In a 1986 poll of the Society for Information Management (mostly MIS directors), William King, a business professor at the University of Pittsburgh, found that 59 percent of the companies had either an irregular process or no formal approach at all for identifying strategic uses of IS (Buday, 1987). What is the decision making policy of managers who are employing IS technology to gain a competitive advantage? How do these managers balance risk and competitive advantage potential? Is return on investment a relevant issue for managers employing IS technology to gain a competitive advantage? What impact does the cost of the project have on a manager's decision to invest? These are the types of concerns that need to be addressed.

The following discussion of research dealing with R&D project selection provides further justification for the factors included in the model, levels of the factors, and the models which are tested.

FACTORS

Risk, Return on Investment and Cost

Many studies have dealt with the positive relationship that exists between the return on an investment and the risk associated with that investment. Bettis defined risk as a manager's subjective judgment of the personal and organizational consequences that result from a specific decision or action (Bettis, 1983). For the purpose of this research, risk is the manager's subjective judgment of the probability of failure of the project under consideration. Return on investment is defined as the marginal (additional) income that can be directly attributed to the IS project divided by the cost of the project. Cost is the estimated total amount to be invested in the project. Researchers have suggested that return and risk are relevant criteria for evaluating R&D projects and new product proposals (Souder, 1975; Wallace, 1983). It seems logical that these factors would be relevant in the decision to invest in an IS project.

Basically, for a given investment, as the amount of return increases so does the amount of risk; everything else remaining the same. Keeping this basic relationship in mind, it is interesting to study the impact of the type of IS technology project (whether the potential to offer a competitive advantage is moderate or high) and the cost of the project on the amount of risk that would be tolerated.

Souder did research in the project selection process of several industrial organizations. He used an "impact procedure" to consensus rank criteria supplied by the managers who participated in his study. Note that profitability or return on investment, probability of success and amount invested were among the top three criteria in all of the studies (Souder, 1975). Clearly these three factors are still considered relevant to the decision to invest in IS technology.

Potential to Offer Competitive Advantage by IS Project

A study by Stahl and Harrell (1983) at an Air Force R&D laboratory showed that the laboratory studied had two operative goals, technical merit and Air Force need, that were relevant to a project resources allocation decision process. Technical merit involved the extent to which the project provided a new or better technical capability to the Air Force. This might suggest that managers value projects that provide the organizations with a competitive advantage.

Porter (1985) defined "competitive advantage" as the mechanism by which a firm "creates and sustains superior performance and is given a way to outperform its rivals" (Porter, 1985). Thus, the competitive advantage potential of an information system project is the degree to which the project will provide the firm with a way to outperform its rivals.

Levels of Factors

Wallace reported on a study by Brooks (1979) which revealed that managers were normally not willing to consider projects that had one or more criteria with strongly negative values. In a study of R&D project selection policies, Wallace noted that by having all the cues at an adequate or better level "the exercise more closely resembles the optimistic flavor of actual product development project proposals" (Wallace, 1983). For these reasons, the factors are considered at only two levels (moderate and high) in this research.

HYPOTHESES

The literature review indicates that researchers and practitioners are interested in managing information systems technology to gain a competitive advantage. The questions naturally arise: Why have some firms been more successful than others in creating a competitive advantage utilizing IS technology? Do these managers have serendipity? What are the relevant criteria utilized by managers as they evaluate IS projects?

Thus, this research analyzes the relevant influence of four factors on the manager's recommendation to invest in IS technology and specifically tests the following five hypotheses. The first two hypotheses relate to comparisons of managers within the same firm (intrafirm) and the last three hypotheses make comparisons between managers in different firms. The hypotheses can be stated in null form as follows:

H1A: There is no statistically significant effect on the manager's recommendation to invest that is explained by the cost, risk, competitive advantage potential, and return on investment associated with an IS project.

H1B: There is no statistically significant effect on the manager's recommendation to invest that is explained by the cost, risk, competitive advantage potential and return on investment associated with an IS project and interaction terms made up of the product of these cues with other cues.

H2: There is no statistically significant difference between the manager's subjective weights and the relative weights obtained from the regression model.

H3: There is no statistically significant association between the cue weights of the individual models and the use of information systems technology.

H4: The cue weights are not significantly related to the performance of a firm.

H5: There is no statistically significant difference between the weights placed on the various cues across industry categories.

RESEARCH METHODOLOGY

Operationalization of Variables

The variables were operationalized by using a decision making exercise. This exercise presented various scenarios to managers involved in strategic planning. The scenarios were developed by varying the levels of each of the four factors. Each manager evaluated each scenario independently. The relative weights placed on each factor by the managers were then determined. A model was formulated for each manager and comparisons made among models. A determination was made of the activity level of the manager's firm in the use of information systems technology by evaluating the participant's response to a list of questions on the instrument designed for this purpose.

Experimental Design

The experimental design was a $2 \times 2 \times 2 \times 2$ full factorial experiment. The four predictor variables measured were the cues (return on investment, risk, cost and potential to offer a competitive advantage) previously identified and defined. The variables were defined in the beginning of the exercise as follows.

"Note: Competitive advantage potential is the extent to which the project will provide the firm with a way to outperform its rivals. Cost is the total amount invested in the project. Return on investment is the marginal (additional) profit that can be directly attributed to the IS project divided by the cost of the project. Risk is the probability of *failure* of the project."

Each of these independent variables had two levels: moderate and high. Sixteen hypothetical situations (or experimental conditions) were described by changing the values of each of the four cues. The response variable represented the manager's recommendation to invest or not invest based on the four cues. The relative weights in the models describe the relative importance to the response variable.

Figure 10.1
Example: Information System Project

```
                         IS PROJECT #X

COST................................................HIGH

RISK............................................MODERATE

IS COMPETITIVE ADVANTAGE POTENTIAL..............MODERATE

ROI.............................................MODERATE


Indicate below your recommendation regarding approval or
disapproval of this project for funding.

-5    -4    -3    -2    -1    0    +1    +2    +3    +4    +5

Strongly                                          Strongly
Recommend                                         Recommend
Disapproval                                       Approval
```

The Information System Decision Making Exercise

Each decision maker was asked to evaluate each scenario related to an information system project and decide whether to recommend investment in the project. Figure 10.1 contains a sample of the instrument.

Information Systems Technology Activity Index

The last page of the instrument contained questions which were used in the information systems technology activity index. The intent of these questions was to measure the extent of information systems technology usage within a firm. These questions were adapted from a profile which appeared in *Business Week* (Harris, 1985). The questions are in Figure 10.2.

The Sampled Planners

The instrument was sent to a random sample of 1,000 members of The Planning Forum—The International Society for Planning and Strategic Management. A recent brochure of this organization states that the membership of the Planning Forum focuses on "planning and strategic management tools in realizing superior corporate performance." The Planning Forum monitors new developments in planning and strategic management, conducts research, and evaluates complementary and conflicting information. The membership of this organization includes board members, CEOs, line and staff executives, academicians and representatives of the world's

Figure 10.2
Information Systems Technology Activity

Please answer the following questions by responding yes/no to
indicate whether your firm has activity in the following areas:

		Yes	No
1.	Does your firm's sales force test cold leads by telephone first to determine the best prospects?	---	--
2.	Does your firm allow customers to use your firm's data base to track orders and shipments?	---	--
3.	Does your company use videodisks or other computer-aided instruction techniques to train workers?	---	--
4.	Do sales personnel utilize portable computers to enter orders directly and get messages?	---	--
5.	Has your company set up a computer link between your treasurer's office and the bank to obtain financial information?	---	--
6.	Has your firm supplied customers with a toll free number for consumer questions and complaints?	---	--
7.	Does your firm keep computerized data on competitive firms? e.g. automated databases with costs, prices, etc.	---	--
8.	Has your firm utilized information systems technology to automate oeprations? e.g. use of Robotics, CAD/CIM, etc.	---	--
9.	Has your company created exclusive computer communications with customers for order entry and exchange of product?	---	--
10.	Does your company offer to develop new services for outsiders by using off-peak processing power?	---	--

(This list of information technology areas was adapted from an
article by Catherine Harris, which appeared in <u>Business Week</u>,
1985.)

---

leading consulting firms specializing in business planning. Each member of
the sample was mailed a cover letter explaining the decision making exercise, and a postage-paid return envelope. Two hundred ninety-one usable
responses were received from the 1,000 decision making exercises sent out.

RESULTS

An individual regression on the four main effects was performed for each
completed exercise. Each respondent's individual model was tested for

internal consistency. This meant that the R^2 for each respondent's individual model had to be greater than .48 at the .05 significance level. Only ten respondents were inconsistent in evaluating information systems technology projects. Those ten were deleted from further analysis. The mean R^2 of the individual regression models was 0.81 with a minimum of 0.52 and a maximum of 1.00.

Hypotheses 1

The first hypothesis tested whether the cost, return, risk and the competitive advantage potential of an information systems project (singularly or combined) were statistically significant factors is the decision to invest in an IS systems project. Group regression models were developed using the four main effects, and the four main effects with the six interactions. Individual regression models were also developed for each respondent. An analysis was made of the frequency of significant responses for each of the four cues, and for each of four cues with the six interaction terms. The total relative weights for all interaction terms was 1.55 percent. No single interaction term had a relative weight greater than 1.0 percent. These results suggested that the additive main effects model better explained the decision making behavior of the managers.

Table 10.1 summarizes the results of the group regression model developed using only the four main effects. The respondents' decisions were pooled to develop this model. All four main effects were significant at the .01 level. Table 10.2 summarizes the results of the frequency of significant

Table 10.1
Group Regression with Four Main Effects

FACTOR[a]	Standardized Estimate	Relative Weight (%)	t
Cost	-0.24	10.76	-23.02*
Risk	-0.42	33.81	-40.82*
ISCAP	0.39	29.73	38.27*
ROI	0.37	25.70	35.59*

*p < .01.

R^2 = 0.52.

[a]ISCAP is Information System Competitive Advantage Potential.

ROI is Return on Investment.

Note: n = 4,496.

Table 10.2
Statistically Significant Individual Models

Types of Models[a]	Number of Respondents
4 Factors	73
3 Factors Statistically Significant	
COST, RISK, ISCAP	16
RISK, ISCAP, ROI	56
COST, ISCAP, ROI	7
COST, RISK, ROI	9
2 Factors Statistically Significant	
COST, RISK	7
COST, ISCAP	4
COST, ROI	7
RISK, ISCAP	21
RISK, ROI	12
ISCAP, ROI	31
Single Factor	
COST	1
RISK	18
ISCAP	9
ROI	10
TOTAL	281

Note: ISCAP was significant for 217 Respondents.
       RISK   "   "   " 212   "   .
       ROI   "   "   " 205   "   .
       COST   "   "   " 124   "   .

[a]ISCAP is Information System Competitive Advantage Potential.

ROI is Return on Investment.

responses for each of the four cues from the individual models. Both tables indicate that risk, information systems competitive advantage potential and return on investment were the three most important factors.

Hypothesis 2 represents a test of whether decision makers have good insight into their own decision making. Four paired t-tests examined the differences between the subjective weights and the relative weights of the decision makers in Table 10.3. The results show the same lack of insight into multiple criteria decision making observed in other chapters.

Hypothesis 3 explores whether the relative weights were related to the use of information system technologies for strategic purposes. Correlation coefficients of each relative weight with respondents' scores from the Information

Table 10.3
Comparison of Average Relative and Subjective Weights

Factor	Subjective Weight	Relative Weight	Difference	t
Cost	20.41	11.63	8.78	12.76*
Return on Investment	27.19	27.45	-0.26	- 0.24
Competitive Advantage Potential	28.11	29.31	-1.20	0.27
Risk	24.22	31.55	-7.34	- 5.50*

*p < .01.

Note: n = 281.

Systems Technology Activity Index (ISTAI) were computed. For the entire sample, none of those four correlations were significant. However, an analysis by industry showed some significant results (Table 10.4). The correlation of the relative weight of risk with ISTAI was statistically significant in the chemical industry and in the consulting industry. The relative weight placed on cost was significantly correlated with ISTAI in the electrical and electronics industry. The relative weight placed on competitive advantage potential was significantly correlated with ISTAI in the non-bank financial industry, the banks and holding companies and in miscellaneous manufacturing.

Hypothesis 4 tests whether the relative weights decision makers place on the cues are significantly related to the firm's performance. Respondents were asked to report financial data. This research used return on sales (ROS) and return on assets (ROA) as measures of performance. Correlation coefficients of each relative weight with each performance measure were computed. For the entire sample, none of the eight correlations were significant. An analysis by industry revealed that there was a statistically significant correlation between the relative weight placed on cost and one of the two performance measures in the electrical, publishing/radio and TV, and savings and loan industries. The relative weight placed on competitive advantage potential and performance was statistically significant in the chemicals, and non-bank/financial industries. The correlation between the relative weight placed on return on investment and performance was statistically significant in the food processing industry. These results appear in Table 10.5.

Table 10.4
Correlation of Relative Weights with ISTAI by Industry

INDUSTRY	N	COST	RISK	ISCAP[a]	ROI[a]
Automotive	8	-.08	.21	-.52	.53
Banks & Holding Cos.	31	-.06	.26	.63*	.28
Chemicals	9	.13	.71**	-.46	-.65
Drugs	8	.18	-.25	.28	-.07
Electrical & Electronics	8	.79**	-.22	-.04	.12
Food Processing	8	-.45	.32	-.59	.32
Utilities	22	.38	-.09	-.32	.27
Nonbank Financial	23	.11	-.11	.48**	.23
Office Equipment	9	-.55	.29	-.37	.26
Publishing Radio & TV	6	-.10	-.36	-.15	.42
Retailing/Nonfood	6	-.25	-.38	.01	.19
Savings & Loan	5	-.55	.34	-.55	.18
Service	25	-.01	-.20	.29	-.02
Misc. Mfg.	16	-.48	-.23	.50**	.15
Natural Resources	9	.26	-.13	-.66	.50
Education/Research	8	.12	.12	-.10	-.14
Consulting	19	-.00	.58*	-.17	.36
Health Care	7	.18	.37	-.47	.03

*p < .01.
**p < .05.
Note. Business Week's Categories with N > 5.
[a]ISCAP is Information System Competitive Advantage Potential.
ISTAI is Information System Technology Activity Index.
ROI is Return on Investment.

Hypothesis 5 tests whether decision makers place different weights on the cues based on the principal industry in which their firm operates. This was done by asking respondents to identify their firm's major industrial category on a list of 38 industries obtained from *Business Week's* 1984 Scoreboard. Four analyses of variance (ANOVA) were performed to test for significant differences in means of the relative weights across industry

Table 10.5
Correlations of Relative Weights with Performance Across Industries

INDUSTRY	N	COST	RISK	ISCAP[b]	ROI[b]
Automotive	7	-.22	.12	.42	-.30
		-.57	-.05	.46	.27
Banks	20	.35	.18	-.27	-.18
		.30	-.00	-.07	.11
Chemicals	7	-.26	.47	-.83**	.20
		.01	.51	-.88*	.05
Drugs	7	.00	.00	.00	.00
		-.03	-.58	.48	.13
Electrical	8	-.37	.43	-.14	-.23
		-.70**	.19	-.12	.05
Food Processing	6	-.65	-.48	-.20	.81**
		-.57	.18	-.57	.57
Utilities	16	.21	.09	.01	-.27
		-.41	.17	.28	-.34
Nonbank/Financial	20	.39	-.21	.24	-.08
		.26	-.33	.47**	-.02
Office Equipment	9	-.11	.60	-.28	-.23
		-.09	.18	-.06	-.08
Publ. Radio/TV	3	-.99**	-.88	.79	.52
		.00	.00	.00	.00
Retailing	6	.18	-.75	.56	-.50
		-.71	.06	.37	-.41
Savings & Loan	3	-1.0**	.31	-.61	.28
		.13	.26	.39	.04
Service	18	.10	.12	-.25	.09
		.07	.35	-.25	-.11
Misc. Mfg.	15	-.23	-.17	.11	.30
		-.24	-.03	.00	.22
Natural Resources	9	0.00	.38	-.16	-.22
		-.34	.38	-.32	.02
Consulting	16	-.38	-.02	.30	-.02
		-.43	-.09	.30	.06
Health Care	5	.50	-.44	.10	.55
		.76	-.57	.15	.56

*p < .01.
**p < .05.
Note. Business Week's Categories with N > 3.
[a]The first row for each industry contains the correlations with Return on Sales. The second row contains the correlations with Return on Assets.
[b]ISCAP is Information System Competitive Advantage Potential. ROI is Return on Investment.

categories. These results are shown in Table 10.6. No significant differences were noted.

Another analysis was performed to test for differences in vectors of means for the Information System Technology Activity Index (ISTAI) across industry categories. It is interesting to note that there were significant differences in the degree of usage of information systems technology as measured by ISTAI across industry categories. These results are shown in Table 10.7.

Table 10.6
Comparison of Relative Weights Across Industries

INDUSTRY	N	COST	RISK	ISCAP[a]	ROI[a]
Automotive	8	13.87	35.75	33.12	17.25
Banks & Holding Cos.	31	13.93	30.74	29.29	26.12
Chemicals	9	10.77	33.22	31.88	24.22
Drugs	8	8.75	40.12	26.62	24.50
Electrical & Electronics	8	7.00	30.00	32.87	30.00
Food Processing	8	14.25	31.12	25.62	28.87
Utilities	22	11.72	32.50	25.00	30.77
Nonbank Financial	23	12.34	33.30	20.95	32.91
Office Equipment	9	7.33	25.88	38.44	28.44
Publishing Radio & TV	6	12.00	24.33	37.00	26.66
Retailing/Nonfood	6	3.16	15.50	43.83	37.50
Savings & Loan	5	8.00	37.40	19.20	35.40
Service	25	11.68	36.08	27.48	25.16
Misc. Mfg.	16	15.25	40.00	22.00	22.75
Natural Resources	9	11.00	17.55	36.44	35.00
Education/Research	8	13.65	35.12	30.00	21.25
Consulting	19	14.21	26.84	31.10	27.94
Health Care	7	16.57	38.28	23.85	21.28
ANOVA F		.72	.78	.99	.58

Note: Business Week's Categories with $N > 5$.
[a]ISCAP is Information System Competitive Advantage Potential.
ROI is Return on Investment.

CONCLUSION

This empirically based research provided insight into the decision making process of managers faced with the decision of whether or not to invest in an information systems technology project which offers the firm the potential to gain a competitive advantage. There is evidence that some firms have

Table 10.7
Comparison of Information System Technology Activity Index Across Industries

INDUSTRY	N	MEAN
Automotive	8	5.12
Banks & Holding Cos.	31	4.50
Chemicals	9	3.22
Drugs	8	6.50
Electrical & Electronics	8	4.25
Food Processing	8	5.37
Utilities	22	5.00
Nonbank Financial	23	5.39
Office Equipment	9	5.11
Publishing Radio & TV	6	4.50
Retailing/Nonfood	6	4.66
Savings & Loan	5	5.50
Service	25	3.68
Misc. Mfg.	16	5.75
Natural Resources	9	3.66
Education/Research	8	1.87
Consulting	19	3.21
Health Care	7	4.40
ANOVA F		2.07*

$*p < .01.$
Note: Business Week's Categories with $N > 5$.

been more aggressive than others in the use of IS technology for strategic purposes. This research also compared the decision making models of managers in these firms with managers from less aggressive firms.

The most important finding is that these 281 executives from a variety of industries placed about 30 percent of their weight in making a decision to fund a new project on the information system competitive advantage potential

(ISCAP) of the project. This was separate from the weight that they placed on traditional measures like return on investment and risk. For the sake of gaining a competitive advantage through the use of new information technologies, they were willing to experience a more modest return on investment.

Correlations of the four cue weights with performance by industry yielded some significant findings. In general, the more weight that the decision makers placed on cost in their information system project funding decision, the lower was the firm's profitability. Also, the more weight placed on return on investment of the IS project, the higher was the firm's performance. The associations between weight on information system competitive advantage potential and firm profitability were mixed. In some firms, the lower the weight on ISCAP, the higher was the performance. In some, the higher the weight on ISCAP, the higher was the firm performance. More research into these fascinating mixed findings is needed.

Differences in the use of information systems across industry were also observed. Using an Information System Technology Activity Index (ISTAI) published in *Business Week*, it was observed that the educaton/research industry scored the lowest on ISTAI, whereas the drug industry scored the highest. Given the variances observed on ISTAI by industry and the variances observed among the individual decision makers, it would not be surprising to see even more pronounced differences among firms in the future on the use of information technology to gain a competitive advantage.

REFERENCES

Bettis, R. A. "Modern Financial Theory, Corporate Strategy, and Public Policy: Three Conundrums." *Academy of Management Review*, 1983, 8 (3), 406–415.

Blumenthal, Sherman C. *MIS: A Framework for Planning and Development*. Englewood Cliffs, N.J.: Prentice-Hall, 1969.

Brooks, T. L. "Policy Capturing of Management Personnel Through Project Selection Decision Making in an Air Force R & D Laboratory." M.S. Thesis, Air Force Institute of Technology, Dayton, Ohio, 1979.

Buday, Robert S. "Quicksand—What Kills Strategic Systems." *InformationWEEK*, 1987, 116.

Cash, James I., Jr., and Konsynski, Benn R. "IS Redraws Competitive Boundaries." *Harvard Business Review*, March-April 1985.

Gibson, Cyrus F., and Nolan, Richard L. "Managing the Four Stages of EDP Growth." *Harvard Business Review*, January-February 1974.

Harris, Catherine. "Information Power—How Companies are Using New Technologies to Gain a Competitive Edge." *Business Week*, October 14, 1985.

Holloway, Clark. "Strategic Management and Artificial Intelligence." *Long Range Planning*, October 1983.

IBM Corporation. *Business Systems Planning: Information Systems Planning Guide*. Application Manual GE 20-0527-1, August 1975.

Janulaitis, M. Victor. "Gaining Competitive Advantage." *InfoSystems*, October 1984, 56–58.

Kantrow, A. ""The Strategy-Technology Connection." *Harvard Business Review*, July-August 1980, 6–21.

Keen, Peter G. W. "Value Analysis: Justifying Decision Support Systems." *Management Information Systems Quarterly*, March 1981, 1–14.

King, William R., and Cleland, David I. "A New Method for Strategic Systems Planning." *Business Horizons*, August 1975.

Kriebel, Charles H. "The Strategy Dimensions of Computer Systems Planning." *Long Range Planning*, September 1968.

Lucas, Henry C., Jr. *Information Systems Concepts for Management*. New York: McGraw-Hill, 1982.

McFarlan, F. Warren. "Problems in Planning the Information System." *Harvard Business Review*, May-June 1971.

McFarlan, F. Warren. "Portfolio Approach to Information Systems Administration." *Harvard Business Review*, September-October 1981.

McFarlan, F. Warren. "Information Technology Changes the Way You Compete." *Harvard Business Review*, May-June 1984.

McFarlan, F. Warren. *The Information Systems Research Challenge Proceeding*. Cambridge Mass.: Harvard Business School Press, 1984.

McFarlan, F. Warren, McKenney, James L., and Pyburn, Philip. "Information Archipelago: Charting the Course." *Harvard Business Review*, January-February 1983.

McKenney, James L., and McFarlan, F. Warren. "The Information Archipelago—Maps and Bridges." *Harvard Business Review*, September-October 1982.

McLean, Ephraim R., and Soden, John V. *Strategic Planning for MIS*. New York: John Wiley & Sons, 1977.

Nolan, Richard L. "Managing the Crisis in Data Processing." *Harvard Business Review*, March-April 1979.

Parsons, Gregory L. "Information Technology: A New Competitive Weapon." *Sloan Management Review*, Fall 1983.

Peters, Thomas J., and Waterman, Robert H., Jr. *In Search of Excellence: Lessons From America's Best Run Companies*. New York: Harper & Row, 1982.

Porter, Michael E. "How Competitive Forces Shape Strategy." *Harvard Business Review*, March-April 1979.

Porter, Michael E. *Competitive Strategy: Techniques for Analyzing Industries and Competition*. New York: The Free Press, 1980.

Porter, Michael E. *Competitive Advantage*. New York: The Free Press, 1985.

Porter, Michael E., and Millar, Victor E. "How Information Gives You Competitive Advantage." *Harvard Business Review*, July-August 1985.

Rockart, John F., and Treacy, Michael E. "The CEO Goes On-Line." *Harvard Business Review*, January-February 1982.

Rockart, John F. "Chief Executives Define Their Own Data Needs." *Harvard Business Review*, March-April 1979.

Schoen, Donald R. "Managing Technological Innovation." *Harvard Business Review*, May-June 1969.

Souder, W. E. "Achieving Organizational Consensus with Respect to R & D Project Selection Criteria." *Management Science*, February 1975.

Souder, W. E. "Comparative Analysis of R & D Investment Models." *AIIE Transactions*, March 1972.

Stahl, Michael J., and Zimmerer, T. W. "Modeling Product Development Decision Policies of Managers and Management Students: Differences Between Subjective and Relative Weights." *IEEE Transactions on Engineering Management*, February 1983.

Stahl, Michael J., and Harrell, Adrian M. "Identifying Operative Goals by Modeling Project Selection Decisions in Research and Development." *IEEE Transactions on Engineering Management*, November 1983.

Vincent, David R., "Information on the Bottom Line." *Computerworld*, 1984, 18, 25–32.

Wallace, Stanley E. "Policy Capturing and Delphi: An Experiment in Improving Concensus of R&D Project Selection Policies in an Industrial Organization." Ph.D. diss., Clemson University, 1983).

Whisler, Thomas L., and Leavitt, Harold J. "Management in the 1980's." *Harvard Business Review*, November-December 1985.

PART III

Strategic Decisions Within Firms

The studies reported on in the previous chapters included data from many firms. In some cases, the data were across industries. This part of the book deals with two separate studies which were each conducted within a single firm. The implications for practice are most relevant for the strategic planners and executives within a firm who must be concerned with the progress of strategic planning.

Chapter 11 shows how decision modeling was used within a firm to measure the amount of disagreement among the relevant decision makers concerning which future strategies the firm should pursue. This may be particularly relevant in a firm where disagreement seems to exist among multiple decision makers on strategic direction. This is doubly important since the same lack of insight into the strategic decisions was observed here as in Chapters 2, 7 and 10. How can executives resolve their disagreements if they cannot articulate what is important in strategic direction?

Chapter 12 examines an important business-level decision in a high-tech firm, that is, the decision on which development projects to fund. The chapter also presents data which show how feedback of data on other decision makers in the firm can change a decision maker's policy. Again, a lack of insight into decisions was demonstrated.

CHAPTER 11

Strategic Planning Within a Firm: Modeling Disagreement on Strategies

STRATEGY FORMULATION

The strategic management process has been traditionally broadly divided into the formulation of strategy and its implementation. The process of strategy formulation has been traced and outlined by such notable authors as Andrews (1971), Ansoff (1965), Christensen, Berg and Salter (1980), Hofer and Schendel (1978), and Pearce and Robinson (1982). Snow and Hambrick remarked that an advantage of distinguishing between strategy formulation and strategy implementation is that "the cognitive aspects of strategy formulation can be viewed as an important phase apart from the action component implementation" (1980, p. 528).

This chapter deals with the application of a methodology which examines the cognitive aspects of the last stage of the strategy formulation process-strategic choice. It seems intuitive to say that strategic implementation will be improved if a higher level of consensus regarding strategic choice is attained prior to implementation. What becomes most critical is the organizational consequence of a strategy which has not captured the real inputs of each key player regarding his or her interpretation of the priorities of strategic choices. The result can be strategy approved unanimously, but supported in its implementation with less than full and complete commitment.

Henry Mintzberg (1979) described five internal coalitions: peak coordinators, middle-line managers, operators, support staff and analysts. The

This chapter was written by Michael J. Stahl and Thomas W. Zimmerer of Clemson University. An earlier version of this chapter received an Honorable Mention Award for the Best Paper in Corporate and Organizational Planning at the National Academy of Management Meeting, Boston, August 1984.

peak coordinators primarily interact with the formal conditions of external coalitions. In the organization where we conducted our research, the internal relationship would be best described by Mintzberg as the Command Power Configuration. Although the organization has a few outside directors, all ownership of the business is held internally and, for the most part, concentrated in the hands of the more senior managers and executives. The external coalitions are quite passive and the top management committee (peak coordinators) are the central and dominant force in the formulation of corporate strategy. One would assume that an organization whose goal formulation was so centralized would produce a high degree of consensus that was created by such insulated strategic formulation processes. The second research goal was to examine the insight of the executives into their strategic decision making processes.

We were asked by the chief corporate planner of a medium-sized privately held engineering design firm in the southeast to help examine strategic options available to the firm. The firm was already investigating several different strategies. However, the chief planner wanted to obtain the judgments of all the principals in the firms before proceeding further with the efforts. He had heard of some of the authors' work concerning analyzing strategic alternatives via decision modeling (Stahl and Zimmerer, 1984) and wanted to pursue such an approach rather than risk the biases possible in face-to-face interviews or traditional attitude and opinion questionnaires (see Chapter 1). Also, he hoped to quantify the disagreement on the strategies.

METHOD

The Firm's Executives

The president, vice-presidents and division chiefs of the firm were asked to complete the decision making exercise. Twelve of 17 complied. It must be recognized that not only do these 12 individuals have the formal authority for operating the firm, but they also own a majority equity control. Their interest in the future of the firm is more than a trivial concern.

The Planning Decision Making Exercise

This research assumes that strategy consists of at least two major classes of decisions. First, the firm decides which strategy(ies) to pursue. This policy formulation decision is the focus of this research. Second, the firm decides how to implement the strategy(ies). This second decision may be regarded as policy implementation and is not the focus of this study.

The corporate planner and his staff listed, and defined in terms applicable to the firm, the six major strategies or areas which the firm was considering. The firm was already exploring the first four strategies in an exploratory fashion and was considering expanding those strategies. The last two strategies were receiving initial consideration. Although some may not consider a few of these criteria to be corporate strategies, they are the areas wherein the firm was considering long-term allocation of substantial resources.

Based on these six criteria, a simulated decision exercise was constructed. The exercise was designed around a one-half replicate of a full factorial experimental design with the 6 criteria at 2 levels of measurement each for a total of 32 decisions per subject ($1/2 \times 2 \times 2 \times 2 \times 2 \times 2 \times 2$). The first 4 criteria were described as either present or expanded in the plan; the last 2 were either yes or no. A fractional factorial was used to design an instrument of reasonable length and preserve the orthogonality of the criteria. Figure 11.1 contains an example from the decision exercise including the firm's definitions. Subsequent to the example long-range plan, 32 hypothetical plans were randomly presented in the exercise.

Figure 11.1
Example: Long-Range Plan #X

COMPUTER AIDED DESIGN/DATA PROCESSING. Automating and standardizing technical analysis, design and management systems to increase productivity. Capital should be applied to equipment acquisition, software development, and related training......................PRESENT

DIVERSIFICATION (LARGE). Pursuing large projects in high-capital process industries, such as petrochemicals and synfuels, through joint ventures with compatible engineering and design/build firms. Capital should be applied to developing large technical centers......PRESENT

DIVERSIFICATION (SMALL). Pursuing small projects in multiple low-capital industries, such as pharmaceuticals, designed by special projects teams with emphasis on fewer drawings and price competition. Capital resources should be applied to acquiring experienced technical staff and supporting small regional offices.............EXPANDED

MARKET CONCENTRATION. Increased market share in traditional markets, such as pulp and paper and tobacco, emphasizing increased profit through improved work procedures and productivity. Capital would be applied to systems that would improve productivity..........EXPANDED

DESIGN/CONSTRUCT. Merger with or acquisition by construction firm with sufficient size (physical and financial) to pursue high-capital projects that will maximize our combined unit strengths...........NO

TECHNICAL DEVELOPMENT. Tripling the budget for expanding and improving our technical skills through career pathing and training.....YES

Indicate your recommendation regarding approval or disapproval of this plan for funding.

```
    -5    -4    -3    -2    -1    0    +1    +2    +3    +4    +5
```

Strongly   Strongly
Recommend   Recommend
Disapproval   Approval

After the 33 candidate plans were presented, the subjects were asked to indicate the importance they believe they placed upon each of the 6 criteria by distributing 100 points among them. The most important criterion received the most points, etc. These weights are often referred to as subjective weight (SW_i; see equation 1.3) in the behavioral decision theory literature (Schmitt and Levine, 1977). The regression weights (RW_i; see equation 1.2) are referred to as objective weights since they are objectively computed from the subject's decision making behavior (Darlington, 1968). A comparison of the SW_i with the RW_i provides a measure of self-insight into decision making behavior (Slovic and Lichtenstein, 1971).

Since each subject provided 32 decisions, a regression equation was derived for each subject. Each subject's 32 decisions were regressed on the criteria after the criteria were coded as $+1$ or -1 to preserve orthogonality.

RESULTS

The first step in analyzing the data was to check for the presence of interactions within the decision makers. Based upon human limitations in processing data (Newell and Simon, 1972), only the six main effects and the 15 possible two-way interactions were examined. To check for the two-way interactions, a regression equation was computed for each subject's 32 decisions as a function of the 6 main effects and the 15 two-way effects. Four of the 12 executives exhibited one significant two-way interaction. One exhibited 2 significant two-ways. The interactions were randomly distributed among all possible 15 interactions: there was no preferred or consistent interaction. Additionally, a group regression was computed with all 12 decision makers, 384 decisions, 6 mains, and 15 two-ways. No significant interactions existed. Since there was no preferred interaction, only 4 decision makers with an interaction, and no group interaction, the remainder of the analysis is based upon the 6 main effects. Therefore, the model tested for each subject was equation (1.1) where i was 6 and j was 32.

The second step in analyzing the data was to examine the internal consistency reliability of the decision makers. This was done via an examination of the R^2 resulting from the individual regressions on the six main effects (Stahl and Harrell, 1981). An average R^2 of 0.68 and an R^2 range from 0.41 to 0.89 indicated that the decision makers were internally consistent in the application of their decision policies.

Table 11.1 contains the distributions of the relative weights (equation 1.2) for the 12 decision makers. Two major points are worthy of note in Table 11.1. First, the means indicate that there are two categories of criteria in terms of relative importance. Design/Construct and Technical Development are the two most important criteria. These two are several times more important than the other four criteria which are of negligible importance. Second, the variability in the two most important criteria, as measured by the standard deviations and ranges on the relative weights, is substantial.

Table 11.1
Relative Weights

I.D.#	C.A.D./ D.P.	Divers./ Large	Divers./ Small	Mkt. Conc.	Design/ Const.	Tech. Dev.
1	2	9	2	00	11	77
2	7	4	1	2	57	29
3	4	21	2	00	46	27
4	34	1	00	3	24	39
5	14	00	19	12	32	22
6	00	00	25	7	60	9
7	8	00	14	00	21	57
8	6	00	7	3	54	31
9	3	12	6	1	61	17
10	57	1	16	1	00	26
11	5	1	2	1	47	44
12	9	12	12	9	54	6
Average	12	5	9	3	39	32
Standard Deviation	17	7	8	4	21	20

[a]The criteria definitions are in Figure 11.1.

The variability is indicative of dramatic individual decision making differences. Although Design/Construct and Technical Development are preferred, there is less than perfect consensus on those two criteria.

As a further check on the consensus, the group regression with 384 decisions and the 6 effects was computed. The group R^2 was 0.31, compared to the average individual R^2 of 0.68 from 12 separate regressions. Thus, we see a dramatic increase in unexplained or error variation by fitting a common group model. This is further evidence of individual specific decision policies.

The insight of the 12 executives into their own decision making policies was tested via a comparison of the relative and subjective weights. Table 11.2 contains the distributions of the subjective weights for the six criteria. Two differences are noted between the relative and subjective weights (Tables 11.1 and 11.2). The average subjective weights do not show the clear-cut preference patterns that the relative weights show. The subjective weights are nearly uniformly distributed. Second, it is difficult to make a

Table 11.2
Subjective Weights

I.D.#	C.A.D./ D.P.	Divers./ Large	Divers./ Small	Mkt. Conc.	Design/ Const.	Tech. Dev.
1	25	20	10	10	25	10
2	40	10	10	10	20	10
3	10	30	20	5	25	10
4	10	25	20	20	10	15
5	25	3	7	30	15	20
6	15	15	15	10	20	25
7	30	0	0	10	30	30
8	20	10	20	20	15	15
9	5	20	5	20	30	20
10	5	5	10	30	25	25
11	20	10	10	10	20	30
12	20	22	10	13	20	15
Average	19	14	11	16	21	19
Standard Deviation	10	9	6	8	6	7

[a]The criteria definitions are in Figure 11.1.

statement about consensus since the standard deviations of the subjective weights are all close.

The subjective and relative weights were further compared via six paired sample t-tests. The significant differences noted in Table 11.3 follow a bias pattern noted by Slovic and Lichtenstein (1971) and noted in Chapters 2, 7 and 10. Their literature review consistently found that decision makers tend to understate the importance they claim to give to highly important criteria and to overstate the importance they claim to give to low importance criteria. This pattern is evident in the four significant paired sample t-tests between the subjective and relative weights. Slovic and Lichtenstein (1971) referred to the comparison of the subjective and relative weights as a measure of self-insight, that is, the closer the two, the more insightful the decision maker was to his/her own decision making style. The 12 executives who responded did not demonstrate good insight into their decision making process. However, a lack of insight alone does not demonstrate which set of weights is superior.

Table 11.3
Comparison of Average Relative and Subjective Weights

Criteria[a]	Relative Weight	Subjective Weight	t
C.A.D./D.P.	12	19	0.96
Diversification/Large	5	14	4.97**
Diversification/Small	9	11	0.77
Market Concentration	3	16	5.66**
Design/Construct	39	21	-2.76*
Technical Development	32	19	-2.22*

Note: n = 12

[a]The criteria definitions are in Figure 11.1

*p < .05

**p < .01

To determine which set of weights is superior, the power of each set of weights in explaining the variance in the decisions was examined. The explanatory power of two models was compared. The first model is equation (1.1). The second model is equation (1.3) wherein the subjective weights (SW_i) have replaced the beta weights (B_i) from equation (1.1). The models were compared by using paired sample t-tests. The tests examined which model explained more of the variation in the decision, person by person. The paired sample t-tests blocked on the individual decision makers and, thus, were within-person analyses. The procedure is described in detail in Chapter 2.

Both tests in Table 11.4 demonstrate that the objectively weighted model explains the decisions better than the subjectively weighted model. This statement is true both before and after shrinkage from the sample to the population estimates. Not only did the decision makers have poor insight, but the subjective weights produced weaker models.

DISCUSSION AND CONCLUSION

After analyzing 384 strategic decisions of 12 executives who control and own a medium-sized, privately held engineering design firm, several conclusions are offered.

First, the high standard deviations and wide ranges on the criterion relative weights imply that less than perfect consensus existed on the strategies. The behavior of these decision makers demonstrates that the

Table 11.4
Paired Sample t-Tests of Explained Variation

Model	Average Explained Variation Sample (Population)[a]	t
$Y_j = \sum_{i=1}^{6} (SW_i X_{ij})$	.33 (.31)[b]	
		6.51* (5.23*)
$Y_j = \sum_{i=1}^{6} (B_i X_{ij})$	.68 (.61)[c]	

[a]The sample refers to the decisions provided by an individual for this research. The population refers to all the decisions that an individual could provide by completing the exercise several times. The averages are for all the subjects in this research.

[b]The first two entries are the averages of the squared bivariate correlation coefficients between the strategic decisions and new variables computed as the sum expressed in the Model column.

[c]The third and fourth entries are the averages of the squared multiple correlation coefficients derived from regressions of the decisions on the strategic criteria.

*p < .01, df = 10.

criteria are not equally weighted. However, a different message emerged if one relied upon the subjective weights. This reinforces the notion of simulating the decisions via behavioral decision theory and examining regression weights. Researchers must do more than simply ask executives how they make multiple criteria strategic decisions if they wish to determine how the decision making process operates.

Second, the executives displayed poor insight into their own strategic decision making policies. This was evidenced by four significant differences between what the decision makers said was important and what their decisions indicated was important in the relative weights. This coincides with the lack of insight reported by Slovic and Lichtenstein (1971), and Nisbett and Wilson (1977) in their literature reviews, and the findings of Chapters 2,

7 and 10. Indeed, Nisbett and Wilson remarked: "There may be little or no direct introspective access to higher order cognitive processes. The accuracy of subjective reports is so poor as to suggest that any introspective access that may exist is not sufficient to produce generally correct or reliable reports" (1977, p. 233). The lack of insight implies that one cannot just ask a decision maker what is important in multiple criteria decision making since he or she may not be able to accurately verbalize the answer. Rather, one should record multiple decisions and calculate importance. Since the regression weights explained twice the variance in the decisions that the subjective weights explained, one must argue in favor of the decision modeling approach as a better methodology for measuring the cognitive aspects of strategy formulation.

How important is insight into strategic decision making behavior? Hofer and Schendel recently addressed this issue: "Both practice and theory indicate that no exact calculus yet exists by which strategic decisions can be made. Instead, effective strategy making relies on the creativity, judgment, and insights of the decision maker" (1978, p. 177). Given that insight is so important and the decision makers in the research displayed such poor insight, one wonders if a form of cognitive feedback suggested by Hammond et al. (1977) might be appropriate. They suggested capturing the decision maker's model by analyzing his/her decisions and feeding back the model, as well as the model of other decision makers. In such a fashion, the individual can start to consider, with the aid of the decision analyst, the appropriateness of the various models, the lack of insight, etc.

As part of this research, such cognitive feedback was provided to the executives in a meeting. A few months after the meeting, the firm publicly announced that it was actively pursuing negotiations to merge with a construction firm. Within one year, a merger was completed. Apparently, they were implementing the high relative weight on the design/construct criterion, or the executives had already been thinking about formulating such a strategy when the research was performed. Either way, the merger adds validity to the high relative weight on design/construct.

Third, to our knowledge, this is the first study of policy formulation within a firm via behavioral decision theory. Chapter 2 used behavioral decision theory to analyze a policy implementation issue, that is, which firm to acquire. If Hatten (1979), Hofer and Schendel (1978), Mintzberg (1978) and Shirley (1982) are correct in their suggestions that a useful way to analyze business policy is via strategic decisions, then this strategic decision modeling research may be the start of analyzing strategic policies by simulating strategic decision making behavior.

REFERENCES

Andrews, K. R. *The Concept of Corporate Strategy.* Homewood, Ill.: Dow-Jones-Irwin, 1971.

Ansoff, H. I. *Corporate Strategy.* New York: McGraw-Hill, 1965.

Christensen, E. R., Berg, N. W., and Salter, M. S. *Policy Formulation and Administration.* 8th ed. Homewood, Ill.: Richard D. Irwin, Inc., 1980.

Darlington, R. B. "Multiple Regression in Psychological Research and Practice." *Psychological Bulletin,* 1968, 69, 161-182.

Dawes, R. M. "The Robust Beauty of Improper Linear Models in Decision Making." *American Psychologist,* 1979, 34, 571-582.

Dawes, R. M., and Corrigan, B. "Linear Models in Decision Making." *Psychological Bulletin,* 1974, 81, 95-106.

Hammond, K. R. et al. "Social Judgment Theory: Applications in Policy Formulation." In M. R. Kaplan and S. Schwartz, eds., *Human Judgment and Decision Processes in Applied Settings.* New York: Academic Press, 1977.

Hatten, K. "Quantitative Research Methods in Strategic Management." In D. E. Schendel and C. W. Hofer, eds. *Strategic Management: A New View of Business Policy and Planning.* Boston: Little, Brown, 1979.

Hofer, C. W., and Schendel, D. *Strategy Formulation: Analytical Concepts.* St. Paul: West Publishing Co., 1978.

Hoffman, P. J. "The Paramorphic Representation of Clinical Judgment." *Psychological Bulletin,* 1960, 57, 116-132.

Laughlin, J. E. "Comment on 'Estimating Coefficients in Linear Models: It Don't Make No Nevermind.'" *Psychological Bulletin,* 1978, 85, 247-253.

Mintzberg, H. "Patterns in Strategy Formation." *Management Science,* 1978, 24, 934-948.

Mintzberg, H. "Organizational Power and Goals: A Skeletal Theory." In D. W. Schendel, and C. W. Hofer, eds., *Strategic Management: A New View of Business Policy and Planning.* Boston: Little, Brown, 1979.

Newell, A., and Simon, H. A. *Human Problem Solving.* Englewood Cliffs, New Jersey: Prentice-Hall, 1972.

Nisbett, R. E., and Wilson, T. D. "Telling More than We Can Know: Verbal Reports on Mental Processes." *Psychological Review,* 1977, 84, 231-259.

Pearce, J. A., II, and Robinson, R. B., Jr. *Strategic Management: Strategy Formulation and Implementation.* Homewood, Ill.: Richard D. Irwin, Inc. 1982.

Schmitt, N., and Levine, R. "Statistical and Subjective Weights: Some Problems and Proposals." *Organizational Behavior and Human Performance,* 1977, 20, 15-30.

Shirley, R. C. "Limiting the Scope of Strategy: A Decision-Based Approach." *Academy of Management Review,* 1982, 7, 262-268.

Slovic, P., and Lichtenstein, S. "Comparison of Bayesian and Regression Approaches to the Study of Information Processing in Judgment." *Organizational Behavior and Human Performance,* 1971, 6, 649-744.

Snow, C. C., and Hambrick, D. C. "Measuring Organizational Strategies: Some Theoretical and Methodological Problems." *Academy of Management Review,* 1980, 5, 527-538.

Stahl, M. J., and Harrell, A. M. "Modeling Effort Decisions with Behavioral Decision Theory: Toward an Individual Differences Model of Expectancy Theory." *Organizational Behavior and Human Performance,* 1981, 27, 303-325.

Stahl, M. J., and Zimmerer, T. W. "Modeling Strategic Acquisition Decisions." *Academy of Management Journal,* 1984, 27, 369-383.

CHAPTER 12

Project Selection Decisions, Delphi Feedback and Consensus

LITERATURE REVIEW

Project Selection

Project selection has been a topic of research in management and management science for many years. In 1964, Baker and Pound published a paper which cited over 80 references on project selection dealing with techniques for optimally selecting projects. However, these normative models were apparently not being used by managers in their decision making (Cetron, Martino, and Roepcke, 1967; Souder, 1972; Baker, 1974; Souder, 1978.)

In order to understand the problems associated with the use of normative models for R&D project selection, it is necessary to understand the project selection process. Bradenberg (1966) defined the process as having six stages. First is the generation of a set of project proposals. Next, a review is made of the present projects along with the proposed projects. Following that is a determination of how the projects are going to be evaluated by defining a set of criteria. Once the criteria are established, the projects are evaluated against the criteria. This evaluation then results in the selection of the projects to pursue. The final step is actually a return to the beginning of the process for another cycle of the analysis. Although this definition is a sequential process, all the stages are really in process somewhere in the organization at any given time.

The process gets more complicated when trying to select the criteria used for the evaluation. The more criteria there are, the more complex the decision becomes. Baker reports finding 25 different evaluation criteria mentioned in

This chapter was written by Michael J. Stahl and Stanley E. Wallace of Reliance Electric.

the literature: "It is clear that the R&D project selection decision can be characterized as having multiple criteria with no common, underlying measure" (1974, p. 166). Even if the selection criteria can be made, the problems are not over.

In any R&D project, there are many uncertainties. It is common to categorize these uncertainties as being first technical, then commercial, and finally economic. A project can fail because of problems that develop in any one of these categories (Mansfield, 1968). These uncertainties are so important that Mansfield (1971) defined R&D as a process designed to reduce uncertainty.

It can thus be seen that the R&D project selection process is amorphous and complex. As a result, it does not lend itself well to normative models designed to select or aid in selecting projects. In his review of the literature, Baker summarized the reasons why these normative models have not been accepted by decision makers in organizations:

1. Inadequate treatment of interrelationships between projects.
2. Inadequate treatment of uncertainty.
3. Inadequate treatment of multiple criteria.
4. Inadequate treatment of changing criteria and project parameters over time.
5. Too restricted a view of the decision making process.
6. No consideration for nonuniformity in manpower resources.
7. An inability to maintain a balance with regard to the type of projects being pursued (1974, p. 170).

These issues may be compounded in a group decision making environment.

Group Decision Making

Group decision making involves individuals making judgments which are combined in some manner to arrive at a consensus or group decision. Individuals in the project selection decision making process have available to them certain documented information that contains the objective cues pertinent to the decision. Each individual processes this information to arrive at a single subjective estimate of the success of the project. These subjective estimates can be expected to differ because of a number of phenomena that can occur.

First, each individual's use of the objective cues is likely to differ. This situation can be described by differences in the weights the decision makers put on each cue.

It is also plausible that individuals vary as to how consistently they use the various cues. Some managers may always concentrate on certain predictors of success of a project while other managers may vary as to what criteria they consider. It is not the purpose here to determine why this inconsistent use of information occurs. However, in this type of study, it can be expected and measured. Adelman, Stewart, and Hammond (1975), and Balke, Hammond, and Meyer (1974) both report a large amount of policy inconsistency in studies involving real (as opposed to laboratory) judgments.

Another source of differences in judgment results from the fact that there are also non-quantifiable cues that enter into the system. The effects of these cues can be minimized by carefully identifying and including in the model a set of cues that describe, as accurately and completely as possible, the information that is typically available to the decision maker. By doing this, it is then possible to assume that the effects of these other cues are small and randomly distributed. If this assumption is not met, then the policy models that are empirically determined may not be an accurate description of the decision maker's policy. Brown (1972) found that the policy models of individuals' decisions derived under natural and contrived conditions did not differ significantly. Therefore, simulated decision making conditions can be used to empirically determine an individual's policy model.

By using a carefully designed experiment, it is possible to measure policy differences that can be explained by differences in consistency. Once this is accomplished, it is possible to identify and measure the amount of consensus among a group of individuals.

The Delphi technique has been recommended as a way to increase consensus. Delphi may be particularly relevant if all the decision makers are in one firm.

Delphi Technique

The Delphi technique is a process that was developed by the Rand Corporation as a method of forecasting through the use of a group of experts (Brown, 1972). The implementation of a Delphi process is characterized by anonymous response, iterations with controlled feedback, and statistical summarization of the group's response (Linstone and Turoff, 1975). The anonymity of the response is done so that the participants weigh only the information presented to them and do not consider who supplied the information. The purpose of the iterations is to improve the consensus among the group of experts. In fact, it is this convergence of the opinions of the group which has made it such a powerful tool for situations other than forecasting (Dalkey, 1969).

Recognizing some of the shortcomings of project selection research, the issue of consensus in group decision making, and the issue of cognitive insight into decision making processes, the following hypotheses were investigated.

H1: There is no statistically significant effect on the manager's project ratings that is explained by the individual cues.

H2: There is no statisticallly significant difference between the manager's subjective cue weightings (equation 1.3) and relative weights (equation 1.2).

H3: There is no statistically significant difference among the cue weights calculated for each of the five functional groups which are product engineering, industrial engineering, manufacturing, marketing, and finance.

H4: There is no statistically significant difference between the cue weights of the individual models for those managers who completed the exercise twice but (a) *did not* receive any feedback between the two administrations of the decision making exercise, and (b) *did* receive feedback regarding their individual models and the group models between the two administrations of the decision making exercise.

METHODOLOGY

The Project Selection Exercise

The product development project selection decision making exercise is based on a one-half replicate of a $2 \times 2 \times 2 \times 2 \times 2 \times 2$ factorial experiment. This design yields 32 experimental conditions. Additionally, 8 warmup decisions were included.

The independent variables are the six project selection criteria that were identified from company internal documents and defined in the pre-test phase of this research. A hypothetical project is described by the values of each of these six criteria. The value that each criteria can take is either low or high and is determined from the experimental design. The dependent variable is the manager's rating of the project that is described by the six criteria. This rating is a numerical value which reflects the manager's recommendation as to whether that project should be approved or disapproved for funding.

Figure 12.1 shows two hypothetical project descriptions as they appeared in the product development project selection decision making exercise. The two project descriptions in Figure 12.1 illustrate the dichotomous nature of the six project selection criteria. Time to First Shipment is either more than one year or less than one year. The Internal Rate of Return for the project has been forecast as either adequate or excellent. The Manpower Availability is either adequate or excellent. Customer Growth Rate is either stable or growing. Customer Need is either adequate or strong. Activity by Our Competition is either moderate or aggressive.

It is important to note that there is a definite minimum value of the internal rate of return (IRR) for product development projects which is confidential but known to the managers. Also, an IRR above a certain value is considered suspect and indicates that the financial analysis of the project probably failed to include something important. Thus, an adequate IRR is considered to be 5 to 10 percent above the minimum and an excellent IRR is a value somewhere between the adequate value and the value that triggers the suspicion that the analysis is faulty.

Figure 12.1
Two Hypothetical Project Descriptions

Product Development Project No. 1 is characterized by:

    More than one year before first shipment of this product

    Adequate Internal Rate of Return (IRR)

    Excellent manpower availability for developing this product

    Stable customer's markets

    Adequate customer need for this product

    An anticipation of aggressive activity from our competitors

Circle on the scale below your rating for this project.

    Strongly   Strongly
    Recommend -5 -4 -3 -2 -1 0 1 2 3 4 5   Recommend
    Not Funding   Funding

Product Development Project No. 2 is characterized by

    Less than one year before first shipment of this product

    Excellent Internal Rate of Return (IRR)

    Adequate manpower availability for developing this product

    Growing customer's markets

    Strong customer need for this product

    An anticipation of moderate activity from our competitors

Circle on the scale below your rating for this project.

    Strongly   Strongly
    Recommend -5 -4 -3 -2 -1 0 1 2 3 4 5   Recommend
    Not Funding   Funding

Subjective weights were also gathered by asking the respondents to distribute 100 points across the six criteria in accordance with their importance. The respondents were also asked to indicate their functional area.

The Division's Managers

The project selection exercise was sent to 146 managers in one division of a firm that designs and manufactures industrial electrical equipment. The participants were asked to return the completed exercises within approximately three weeks. When the exercises were returned, they were checked to see that they were complete and that the instructions were followed correctly. Ninety-five useable exercises were returned with a personal ID number, demographic information, functional group, and 40 project ratings.

An important part of this study was to determine what effect the feedback of the policy-capturing results had on the participants. If significant policy differences were identified and individuals compared their criteria weights with group average criteria weights, did they try to change their policies in some way? A study pertinent to this question was made by Rohrbaugh (1979) in which he compared policy feedback to the Delphi technique in a controlled experiment involving undergraduate psychology students. He concluded that policy feedback and the Delphi technique resulted in judgments of equal quality but the policy feedback reduced disagreement much more than the Delphi approach. One way to answer the question about the effects of the feedback is to repeat the experiment but only give the feedback of the results to a portion of the original participants. Schmitt and Levine (1977) strongly recommend this "control group" approach as the only way to identify the effects of the feedback.

The respondents who returned properly completed decision making exercises were randomly divided into two groups. One group was a control group that was asked to complete the decision making exercise a second time before they received any feedback as to the results of the first administration of the exercise. The second group received a detailed report which allowed them to compare their criteria weights with the other individuals' criteria weights and with the group average criteria weights. Thus, each individual receiving the feedback was able to determine how his or her product development project rating policy compared with others in the organization. After the feedback of the results was received this Delphi group was asked to complete the decision making exercise a second time.

RESULTS

The first test was an examination of interaction in the decision models. Equation (1.1) with 6 main effect terms ($i = 6$) and 15 two-way interactions was tested for each decision maker. Of the 95 decision makers, only 13 displayed any statistically significant interactive terms. Those 13 were randomly distributed among the 15 possible interactions. At most, 2 decision makers processed the same interaction. Therefore, the remainder of the analysis was based upon the 6 main effect terms with $i = 6$ and $j = 32$ from equation (1.1).

Table 12.1 contains the beta weights (equation 1.1) for the first round by functional group. The beta weights (vs. relative weights) are used because of mixed signs. The relative weights lose the sign since they are a squared transformation.

Table 12.1.
Average Individual Beta Weights by Functional Group
(First Round)

| Functional Group | Project Selection Criteria [1] | | | | | |
	Time	IRR	Manpwr	Cust Growth	Cust Need	Comp
Prod. Eng. (n=42)	.149	.464	.177	.406	.361	.175
Marketing (n=23)	.197	.376	.089	334	.452	.246
Finance (n=11)	.105[a]	.540	.044[a]	.269	.425	.096[a]
Ind. Eng. (n=10)	.248	.421	.232	.313	.425	-.071
Manufacturing (n=9)	.263	.467	.177	.271	.430	.246
Overall (n=95)	.177	.447	.146	.350	.403	.164

[a]Not significantly different from zero at the .05 level.

[1]The criteria are defined in Figure 12.1.

All but three of the weights tested in Table 12.1 are significantly different from zero. Therefore, H1 is rejected and it is concluded that the cues are associated with the project ratings.

To test H3 for differences among the functional groups, the 10 possible pairs of the 5 functional groups were tested for differences in average beta weights for all 6 cues. Only 5 of the 60 t-tests (10 functional group pairs times 6 cues) showed a significant difference. Therefore, H3 was not rejected and it was concluded that there was no evidence of a difference among the functional groups.

The next step in the analysis was to test for cognitive insight among the decision makers. Using six paired sample t-tests as in Chapter 2 (Table 2.2), the subjective weights were compared to the relative weights. As the two significant differences in Table 12.2 indicate, there was evidence of a lack of insight. What the decision makers said was important (subjective weights) differed from what their decisions indicated was important.

The explanatory power of the subjective weights, relative weights, equal weights and beta weights was compared using a technique similar to that explained in Chapter 2 (Table 2.3). As Table 12.3 indicates, the beta weights fared best. The existence of mixed signs among the beta weights might explain why the beta weights are significantly more powerful than the relative weights.

Tables 12.4 and 12.5 address the issue of whether the feedback changed the decision makers' policies. As Table 12.4 indicates, there was one significant

Table 12.2.
Comparison of Average Subjective and Relative Weights
(First Round)

Criteria	Subjective Weight	Relative Weight	t
Time to First Shipment	10.9	9.2	+1.64
Internal Rate of Return	22.0	29.1	-3.75*
Manpower Availability	11.5	5.7	+7.23*
Customer Growth Rate	20.9	20.7	+0.11
Customer Need	21.8	24.0	-1.45
Activity by Our Competition	<u>12.9</u>	<u>11.3</u>	<u>+1.52</u>
Totals	100.0	100.0	

*p < .01.

Note: n = 95.

change for the control group. There were two significant changes for the Delphi group (Table 12.5).

Additionally, it was noted that 11 of the 22 individuals in the Delphi group had a significant change in their regression models. Only 6 of the 32 regression models in the control group changed. A test of proportions indicated that the first proportion is significantly greater than the second proportion (p < .01). Therefore, based on this proportion test and Tables 12.4 and 12.5, it is concluded that the Delphi group exhibited a greater change than the control group.

To examine if there had been increased consensus associated with the feedback, the variances on the beta weights were examined. The ratio of the variances on the beta weights in the second round, to the variances on the beta weights in the first round, was formed for each of the six criteria. For the control group, none of the six ratios was significant. For the Delphi group, none of the six ratios was significant. Therefore, it was concluded that there was no change in consensus associated with the feedback.

CONCLUSIONS

The basis objective of this research was to model specific decision making policies of managers in an industrial organization and determine if

Table 12.3.
Paired Sample t-Tests of Explained Variation
(First Round)

Model	Average Explained Variation Sample (Population)[a]	Improvement in Population Explained Variation	t
Equal Weights	.50 (.48)[b]	-	-
Subjective Weights	.62 (.60)[b]	+.12*	7.97*
Relative Weights	.71 (.70)[c]	+.10*	7.48*
Beta Weights	.82 (.78)[c]	+.08*	4.62*

H_0: The incremental improvements in adjusted R-squared are not significantly different from zero.

[a]The sample refers to the decisions provided by an individual. The population refers to all the decisions that an individual could provide by completing the exercise several times. The averages are for all the subjects in this research.

[b]Averages of the squared bivariate correlation coefficients between the project selection decisions and new variables computed as the sum from the Model column.

[c]Averages of the squared multiple correlation coefficients derived from regressions of the decisions on the project selection criteria.

*p < .01, df = 93.

feedback of these models can improve consensus among the managers. The analysis was performed on the project selection policies of managers in one division of an industrial equipment manufacturer.

Comparisons of average weights and Chow's F test on pairs of regression models tested for changes in policy. However, consensus is independent of the actual policy. Consensus is descriptive of how much agreement there is

Table 12.4
First and Second Round Average Individual Beta Weights
(Control Group)

| Criteria | Average Individual Beta Weights | | | |
	First Round	Second Round	Difference (2nd-1st)	t
Time to First Shipment	.1885	.1741	-.0144	-.053
Internal Rate of Return	.4288	.4703	+.0415	+1.25
Manpower Availability	.1547	.1465	-.0082	-0.33
Customer Growth Rate	.3664	.4055	+.0391	+1.12
Customer Need	.4193	.3678	-.0515*	-2.10*
Activity by Our Competition	.1479	.1179	-.0300	-1.35

*p < .05.

Note: n = 32.

among the managers' policies. Tests for changes in consensus were performed by testing for changes in weight variances. If the variance of the weights changed from the first round to the second round, then it can be concluded that consensus changed.

Tests for decreases in weight variances were performed on the individual beta weights for the control group and the Delphi group. In all cases, there is no evidence to suggest that consensus improved from the first round to the second round. The Delphi group showed a significant number of policy changes, but it is apparent that these changes did not result in improved consensus.

This research effort demonstrates the ability of a simple linear additive equation to model the project selection policies of managers in an industrial organization. A model specification with two-way interaction terms did not improve the model's ability to explain the managers' decision. It was also found that the beta weight models had more explanatory power than the subjective or equal weight models.

In the search for functional group differences, little evidence was found. Most likely, this result occurred because the consensus within the groups was low.

Table 12.5
First and Second Round Average Individual Beta Weights
(Delphi Group)

	Average Individual Beta Weights			
Criteria	First Round	Second Round	Difference (2nd-1st)	t
Time to First Shipment	.2075	.1631	-.0444	-1.19
Internal Rate of Return	.4356	.5054	+.0698*	+1.88*
Manpower Availability	.1448	.1427	-.0021	-0.06
Customer Growth Rate	.3819	.3090	-.0730*	-1.95*
Customer Need	.4086	.3595	-.0491	-0.91
Activity by Our Competition	.1477	.1732	+.0255	+0.69

*$p < .06$.

Note: n = 22.

The stability of the models over time was quite remarkable. This result certainly validated the policy-capturing technique as an accurate modeling tool for studies in decision making. The fact that the Delphi feedback had little effect on policy consensus could be due to the method used for reporting the first round results. It is unlikely that managers would be affected by the results of the first round unless they carefully studied the first-round report. Unfortunately, the researchers could not control how the feedback reports were used, as the participants were geographically located all over the United States.

The evidence showing the weight for Customer Growth Rate dropping in the Delphi group may have been a result of the deteriorating state of the economy (and the division's business) at the time of the administration of the second round of the decision making exercise. The logistics of the second-round administrations required that the Delphi group receive the first-round report after the control group had returned their second-round exercises. This was done so that the control group could not have access to a first-round report before they completed the second-round exercise. The average time lag of four weeks between the control group responses and the

Delphi group responses may have been long enough to have the changing business conditions (recession) affect their policies. Perhaps feedback of policies, with direction on strategy by management, would have increased consensus. This research indicates that feedback by itself does not increase consensus.

REFERENCES

Adelman, L., Stewart, T. R., and Hammond, K. R. "A Case History of the Application of Social Judgment Theory to Policy Formulation." *Policy Science*, 1975, 6, 137-159.

Baker, N. R. "R&D Project Selection Models: An Assessment." *IEEE Transactions on Engineering Management,* 1974, 21, 165-171.

Balke, W. M., Hammond, K. R., and Meyer, G. D. "An Alternate Approach to Labor-Management Relations." *Administrative Science Quarterly,* 1974, 12, 311-326.

Brandeberg, R. G. "Project Selection in Industrial R&D: Problems and Decision Processes." In M. C. Yovits, ed., *Research Program Effectiveness.* New York: Gordon and Breach, 1966.

Brown, T. R. "A Comparison of Judgmental Policy Equations Obtained from Human Judges under Natural and Contrived Conditions." *Mathematical Biosciences,* 1972, 15, 205-230.

Cetron, M. J., Martino, J., and Roepcke, L. "The Selection of R and D Program Content—Survey of Quantitative Methods." *IEEE Transactions on Engineering Management,* 1967, 14, 4-13.

Dalkey, N. C. "An Experimental Study of Group Opinion—The Delphi Method." *Futures,* September 1969.

Davies, G. B., and Pearson, A. W. "The Application of Some Group Problem-Solving Approaches to Project Selection in Research and Development." *IEEE Transactions on Engineering Management,* 1980, 27, 66-73.

Helmer, O. "Convergence of Expert Consensus Through Feedback." U.S. Department of Commerce, Clearinghouse for Federal Scientific and Technical Information, No. AD 605 522, September 1964.

Linstone, H. A., and Turoff, M. *The Delphi Method—Techniques and Applications.* Reading, Mass.: Addison-Wesley, 1975.

Mansfield, E. *Industrial Research and Technological Innovation.* New York: W. W. Norton & Co., 1968.

Mansfield, E., et al. *Research and Innovation in the Modern Corporation.* New York: W. W. Norton & Co., 1971.

Rohrbaugh, J. "Improving the Quality of Group Judgment: Social Judgment Analysis and the Delphi Technique." *Organizational Behavior and Human Performance,* 1979, 24, 73-92.

Schmitt, N., and Levine, R. L. "Statistical and Subjective Weights: Some Problems and Proposals." *Organizational Behavior and Human Performance,* 1977, 20, 15-30.

Souder, W. E. "Comparative Analysis of R&D Investment Models." *AIEE Transactions* 1972, 4, 57-64.

Souder, W. E. "A System for Using R&D Project Evaluation Methods." *Research Management,* 1978, 21, 29-37.
Wallace, S. E. "Policy Capturing and Delphi: An Experiment on Improving Consensus of R&D Project Selection Policies in an Industrial Organization." Ph.D. diss., Clemson University, 1983.

PART IV

Conclusion

CHAPTER 13

Summary, Conclusions and Executive Implications

This book started with the idea of introducing a rigorous alternative methodological approach for research in strategy. The approach consists of modeling executives' strategic decisions with decision making exercises based on rigorous a priori experimental designs and multiple observations per respondent.

Chapter 1 references other decision modeling studies which have shown that the methodology is free of a social desirability response bias in which a subject gives an answer to the researcher, partly as a function of what the subject thinks is an "acceptable" or "appropriate" answer. That chapter also indicates that such simulated decision making exercises can be used to assess an individual's policy model. Other research has shown that policy models obtained under natural and experimental conditions did not differ significantly.

This chapter summarizes the findings of the preceding chapters, offers some conclusions, discusses executive implications and suggests areas for further research. It is organized into discussion of results concerning the methodology and the strategic decision making process, followed by discussion of the content of the findings with implications for executives, and concludes with implications for future research.

PROCESS

Consistency

Unlike many other research methodologies, decision modeling allows calculation of the internal consistency of each respondent. Typically, the average reliability coefficients associated with decision modeling studies are quite high. Table 13.1 summarizes the reliability statistics from the studies in the preceding chapters.

Table 13.1
Reliability by Chapter

Chapter	Average Individual Reliability	Number of Significant Regressions	Number of Inconsistent Regressions
2	0.80	42	0
3	0.80	158	0
4	0.87	339	4
5	0.92	112	1
7	0.83	184	3
8	0.69	118	0
9	0.74	274	0
10	0.81	281	10
11	0.68	12	0
12	0.82	95	0
TOTAL	0.80	1,615	18

The average individual reliability coefficient of 0.80 from Table 13.1 indicates that the decision makers were quite consistent in completing the decision making exercises. Additionally, the ratio of only 18 inconsistent decision makers out of 1,633 regressions speaks well for the reliability of the approach. This is especially noteworthy when one recalls that these data are summaries from the use of 10 different decision making exercises involving approximately 1,500 executives in many different industries. The ability to spot the 18 inconsistent respondents is a definite methodological advantage of this research approach.

Statistical Rigor

The decision modeling methodology is usually based on rigorous, controlled, statistical experimental designs. These designs facilitate computations of the independent contributions of each of the variables to the decisions and the interactions among variables. Table 13.2 presents a summary of the experimental designs used in the various studies. Table 13.3 contains a summary of the testing for interactions among the variables by chapter.

Table 13.2.
Experimental Design by Chapter

Chapter	Experimental Design
2	1/2 of 2x2x2x2x2x2
3	3x3x3
4	double of 2x2x2
5	2x2x2x2
6	Non-experimental
7	2x2x2x2x2
8	3x3x3
9	1/2 of 2x2x2x2x2x2
10	2x2x2x2
11	1/2 of 2x2x2x2x2x2
12	1/2 of 2x2x2x2x2x2

The data in Table 13.2 indicate that the methodological findings of this book concerning decision modeling are quite robust with respect to experimental design as a variety of experimental designs were used. The designs include three variables each at two levels replicated twice (double of $2 \times 2 \times 2$), four variables each at two levels ($2 \times 2 \times 2 \times 2$), five variables each at two levels ($2 \times 2 \times 2 \times 2 \times 2$), a one-half replicate of six variables each at two levels (1/2 of $2 \times 2 \times 2 \times 2 \times 2 \times 2$), three variables each at three levels ($3 \times 3 \times 3$), and non-experimental historical data. The findings in this book are *not* a function of experimental design.

The data in Table 13.3 indicate that the decision making process is basically linear. There is little evidence of interactive processing of the variables by the decision makers. This indicates that the decision making processes can be accurately modeled by an additive linear model. These results correspond with similar results of other studies referenced in Chapter 1.

Cognitive Insight

Chapter 1 references several studies which reported a lack of insight by decision makers into their own decision making policies. Chapters 2, 7, 10, 11 and 12 checked the cognitive insight of the decision makers. Seventeen of the 27 tests showed a significant difference between what the decision makers claimed was important and what their decisions indicated was important.

Table 13.3.
Interactions by Chapter

Chapter	Number of Significant Individual Interactions/ Number Tested	Number of Significant Group Interactions/ Number Tested
2	8 / 630	0 / 15
3	3 / 158	0 / 1
4	27 / 339	0 / 1
5	21 / 672	2 / 6
7	99 / 1,840	3 / 10
8	4 / 354	0 / 12
9	191 / 4,110	0 / 30
10	28 / 281	2 / 6
11	5 / 180	0 / 15
12	13 / 1,425	0 / 15
TOTAL	399 / 9,989	7 / 111

In each of the tests, the pattern of lack of insight was the same: the decision makers claimed to give more weight than they actually did to low importance criteria, and claimed to give less weight than they actually did to high importance criteria. This is the same pattern documented in the literature. The implication for research in strategy is that direct questioning of decision makers concerning how they weight various criteria in their multiple criteria decisions is subject to definite biases.

Tests of the regression weights versus the subjective weights indicated that the regression weights were always more powerful in explaining the decisions. This is true both before and after shrinkage to allow estimates for explanatory power in the population. Therefore, it appears that the regression weights are the preferred measure of the two in explaining importance of the criteria.

Individual Unit of Analysis

A strength of this approach is that a decision making model is derived for each decision maker. Fortunately, advances in computer science have made it easy to perform a regression equation. Over 1,500 separate regression equations were performed in this research. As the contingency theory of strategy becomes more popular, individual models of strategic decision making should grow in popularity.

CONTENT AND EXECUTIVE IMPLICATIONS

Corporate Strategy Decisions

The most noteworthy content finding from Part I of this book, verified in Chapters 3, 4, 5 and 6, is that executives do not make decisions in accordance with the conglomerate diversification precepts of the Capital Asset Pricing Model. The concept of related diversification seemed to receive much stronger support. This was true whether in an acquisition mode or a divestiture mode. These findings of support for related diversification and rejection of conglomerate diversification coincide with recent articles in *Business Week* on mergers referenced in those chapters. Indeed, Chapter 5 demonstrated that the stock market places a higher value on firms which pursue marketing fit as reflected in higher price earnings ratios being significantly associated with higher marketing fit. Using historical data, Chapter 6 demonstrated that related diversification is associated with higher return on capital, higher sales growth, and lower financial risk than conglomerate diversification.

Chapter 7 on joint ventures indicated that firms pursue that strategy primarily for technology/knowledge acquisition, market penetration, and financial risk minimization. Backward integration and financial return received low weights. It was also observed that market penetration was positively associated with the profitability of the parent, whereas emphasis on financial return by the parent was associated with lower ROI.

Business-Level Strategic Decisions

In both the textile and printing industries, Porter's concept of focus as a separate strategy was upheld in Chapter 8. As hypothesized, focus was given more emphasis in smaller firms. Porter's generic strategies were given additional support in Chapter 9 with high weights placed on differentiation and cost leadership as market entry barriers. The importance of information systems technology as a competitive weapon was highlighted in Chapter 10 by the high weight placed on the information system's competitive advantage potential by executives in approving new projects for funding.

The findings of Chapter 7 indicate that an important reason for firms to pursue joint ventures is technology acquisition. Interviews on a recent trip to China referenced in Chapter 7 support the importance of technology acquisition in Chinese joint ventures. The findings of Chapter 9 on market entry barriers indicate that technology can be used to build market entry barriers by reinforcing cost leadership or differentiation. The high weight placed on competitive advantage potential in approving new information systems technology projects by the planners of Chapter 10 reinforces the notion of using technology to gain a competitive advantage. Porter (1985, p. 169) suggests that technology is useful in building competitive advantage primarily as it results in a cost leadership strategy, or as it results in a differentiation strategy. This notion is different from the views of the referenced Chinese who view themselves so far behind their international trading partners in technology that they seem to view technology as an end in itself. The data in this book and Porter's book argue that technology is a means toward an end. It is left to the reader to decide which view is superior in the longer term.

Strategy Within Firms

Chapter 11 demonstrated that decision modeling of alternative strategies under consideration by a firm could be used as part of the planning process to help quantify the amount and location of disagreement on strategies. This assumes increased importance given the lack of insight documented in Chapters 2, 7, 10, 11 and 12. Chapter 12 demonstrated how feedback of decision policies as in a Delphi process could be used to increase consensus on strategies. The findings suggested that guidance from the top of the organization concerning which strategies are important may be needed to further increase consensus. The value of consensus among strategic planners was documented in Chapter 9 where higher consensus was related to higher firm performance.

FUTURE RESEARCH

There are two areas in which this research methodology in strategy seems to be particularly appropriate. The first is model testing, and the second is study of strategy within firms.

In studies examining existing theories or models in which the proposed variables and their relationship have been specified a priori, it appears that decision modeling offers a rigorous, controlled experimental test of such models. Multiple observations per respondent and a regression equation per executive can provide a robust test of a theory. Tests of the CAPM and Porter's theories in this book are good examples.

Alternately, decision modeling of strategic decisions is not recommended for model-seeking studies. Experimental designs with multiple observations per respondent and treatment of all possible combinations of the variables limit the number of variables which can be studied. Interviews, Likert-scaled questionnaires and analyses of existing data bases are more appropriate for such exploratory research.

Decision modeling can facilitate the study of strategy within a firm. By presenting all decision makers with the same set of decision scenarios involving tradeoffs among multiple criteria, tests for differences among individual decision making models can be pursued. Changes in individual models as a result of some intervention, for example, a policy statement from the chief executive, can also be explored. Consensus within the firm can be easily quantified.

If the study of strategy as a discipline is to advance, and reach levels of rigor and sophistication found in other mature disciplines, methodologically sound approaches are needed. Interviews and historical data bases have several limitations. This book offers a methodologically sound alternative for modeling executives' decisions with rigorous experimentally designed decision making exercises and multiple decisions per executive.

Index

About the Author

MICHAEL J. STAHL is Professor and Head of the Department of Management at Clemson University. His two previous books are *Managerial and Technical Talent* (Praeger, 1986) and *Modern Management Techniques in R&D.*